BY S. J. PERELMAN

Dawn Ginsbergh's Revenge
Strictly from Hunger
Look Who's Talking
The Dream Department
Crazy like a Fox
Keep It Crisp
Acres and Pains
Westward Ha!
Listen to the Mocking Bird
The Swiss Family Perelman
The Ill-Tempered Clavichord
Perelman's Home Companion
The Road to Miltown
The Most of S. J. Perelman
The Rising Gorge
The Beauty Part
Chicken Inspector No. 23
Baby, It's Cold Inside
Vinegar Puss
Eastward Ha!
The Last Laugh

THE
LAST LAUGH

S. J. Perelman

INTRODUCTION BY
PAUL THEROUX

SIMON AND SCHUSTER
NEW YORK

Foreword copyright © 1981 by Cape Cod Scrivners Company
Copyright © 1981 by James H. Mathias, as Executor of the Estate of S. J.
Perelman
All rights reserved
including the right of reproduction
in whole or in part in any form
Published by Simon and Schuster
A Division of Gulf & Western Corporation
Simon & Schuster Building
Rockefeller Center
1230 Avenue of the Americas
New York, New York 10020
SIMON AND SCHUSTER and colophon are trademarks of Simon & Schuster
Designed by Irving Perkins
Manufactured in the United States of America
10 9 8 7 6 5
Library of Congress Cataloging in Publication Data
Perelman, S. J. (Sidney Joseph)
    The last laugh.
    I. Title.
PS3531.E6544L3   814'.52   81-4695
ISBN 0-671-42515-3   AACR2
Portions of this book were previously published as articles in
The New Yorker

Contents

6   Contents

PART TWO

INTRODUCTION

By Paul Theroux

Humorists are often unhappy men and satirists downright miserable, but S. J. Perelman was a cheery soul who, when he flew into one of his exalted rages, seemed to have the gift of tongues. He gave his mockery a bewitching style. In his stories, or feuilletons as he liked to call them, he represented himself as a victimized clown. He was "button-cute, wafer-thin" and reared turkeys ("which he occasionally exhibits on Broadway"); or Dr. Perelman, "small bore in Africa"; or a mixture of Sad Sack and Pierre Loti, haplessly sampling the pleasures of out-of-the-way places; or finally as a sort of boulevardier and roué who, at the moment of sexual conquest, is defeated by a wayward bedspring.

When I first began reading him in the 1950s—I was in junior high school—I was excited by his malicious humor, his huge vocabulary and what I took to be his lunatic fantasy. I sensed a spirit of rebellion in him that stirred the anarchy in my school-boy soul. After I started to travel, it struck me that much of what he wrote was true: Perelman's Africa was the Africa no one else had noticed. His stories were bizarre because he sought out the bizarre. He cherished oddity and, being truly adventurous, was willing to put himself to a lot of trouble to find it (he strolled around Shanghai in 1947 looking for it). Then I met him. He *was* button-cute, and also a bit of a roué, and accident-prone. If he had been writing fantasies, we would think of him as a humorist, a writer of gags, whose object was merely to entertain. But he wrote about the world, and his intensity and his anger made him into a satirist.

A satirist seems a sour and forbidding figure—a mocker, a pessimist, a grudge-bearer, a smirker, something of a curmudgeon, perhaps with a streak of cruelty, who, in inviting the reader to jeer at his victim, never misses a trick or withholds a nudge. How does one suggest that such a man may also have a great deal of charm? Perelman's friends liked him very much. He was generous, he was funny, he was enormously social, he didn't boast. Travel has the effect of turning most people into monologuists; it made Perelman an accomplished watcher and an appreciative listener. When he talked in his croaky drawl he did so in the elaborate way he wrote, with unlikely locutions and slang and precise descriptions diverted into strings of subordinate clauses. He was small and neatly made; he wore very handsome clothes, usually of an English cut; and in his pockets he carried clippings he tore from the newspapers—one he showed me was about the movie *The Texas Chain-Saw Massacre,* which he eventually worked into a story. He read the London *Times* every day (he had an airmail subscription), more, I think, for the unusual names than for anything else. In today's *Times*, Sir Ranulph Twisleton-Wykeham-Fiennes has just reached the South Pole; Captain Sir Weldon Dalrymple-Champneys has just died; and both Miss C. Inch and Miss E. L. F. I. Lunkenheimer have just got married. Perelman welcomed news of this kind.

In his way, he was a man of the world. A man of the world, almost by definition, is never content anywhere. Perelman was a bit like that. He had a great capacity for pleasure, but he was restless, always active, game for anything; he fed himself on change. He began writing at Brown University, where a fellow classmate was Nathanael West (Perelman married West's sister Laura in 1929), and at the age of 25, with the success of his first book, *Dawn Ginsbergh's Revenge*, he was invited to Hollywood to write jokes for the Marx Brothers. He went, and he liked to say that Hollywood reminded him of a novel he had read in Providence as a boy, *In the Sargasso Sea*, by Thomas Janvier (anyone who has the luck to find this 1899 story of marooning and murder in the nightmare swamp will immediately see the connection). From time to time throughout his life, Perelman returned to Hollywood, struggled with scripts and then fought free. At the age of 74, fresh from the travels he recounted in *Eastward Ha!*, he tried to drive his vintage 1949 MG from Paris to Peking, commemorating the trip of Count Something-or-other. It was not such a crazy scheme. He had been around the world a dozen times. He was in good health, his car had recently had a tune-up, he had a generous sponsor and many well-wishers, and he liked to say (though joshing himself with his chain-smoker's chuckle) that he knew Malaysia and Hong Kong like the back of his hand.

In a Thai restaurant, in London, on Christmas Eve, he told me about his drive to Peking. He had just flown in from China. The trip, he said, was a total disaster. The glamour girl he had chosen for navigator had been fired at the outset for selling her story to a magazine. He had quarreled with his fellow drivers all the way through India. There had been kerfuffles with customs men in Turkey. The car was not allowed through Burma and, as there was no room on a ship to Malaysia, the car had been air-freighted to Hong Kong. There were more scenes in Hong Kong. "The others freaked out," Perelman said, but with the old car now parked in Kowloon, he flew to Peking and spent two weeks in a Chinese hospital with a severe case of bronchitis, aggravated by double pneumonia.

"Now I have to write about it," he said. "It'll be horrible."

Frankly, I thought the subject was made for him. Nothing is more Perelmanesque than a marathon drive across the world interlarded with setbacks, blown gaskets, howling Turks and long delays in flea-ridden Indian hotels. And pneumonia in Peking was the perfect ending for someone who always racked his brain for grand finales. (His editor at *The New Yorker*, William Shawn, told me recently, "He always had trouble with endings.") But this last collection of Perelman pieces contains nothing about that Paris to Peking trip. This is odd, because he had made his reputation by describing the complicated orchestration of fiascos.

A month before he died, he wrote me a letter in which he said, "I myself have spent altogether too much time this year breaking my nails on the account of the Paris–Peking trip I made . . . and after a lot of bleeding cuticle, I decided to abandon it. I guess there are certain subjects—or maybe one's subjective reactions to them—that in spite of the most manful attempts are totally unproductive. The one I picked certainly was, and it took a lot of Sturm und Drang to make me realize that my Sisyphean labors were getting me nowhere."

This was the only gloomy paragraph in an otherwise chirpy letter. His letters were long, frequent, and sensationally funny— indeed, so funny that, after receiving a few, Raymond Chandler (always a hoarder and procrastinator where writing was concerned) replied worriedly, warning Perelman against squandering his wit: "You shouldn't give the stuff away like that when you can sell it, unless of course your letters are just rough notes for articles."

But they weren't "just rough notes for articles." They were generous and intelligent expressions of friendship and most of them far too scandalous to be retailed. Here is the opening paragraph of a letter Perelman wrote me on Christmas Eve, 1976:

Between the constant repetition of "White Christmas" and "Jingle Bells" on station WPAT and the increasing frenzy of the Saks and Gimbels newspaper ads as these fucking holidays draw near, I have been in a zombie-like state for weeks, totally incapable of rational thought or action. I must have arrived at near-paralysis yesterday afternoon when I was in the 4th-floor lingerie section ("Intimate Apparel") in Saks 5th Avenue. I had just purchased two such intimate garments for gifties to a couple of ladies of my acquaintance, a tall blonde and a somewhat shorter brunette. For the former, I had chosen a black lace chemise in the style known as a teddy back in the twenties (familiar to you as the scanty garment worn by Rita Hayworth in the wartime pinup). For the shorter brunette, a similar peach-colored job. Both of these real silk, parenthetically, and as I signed the charge slip, I knew that when the bill came in after January 1st, I would kick myself for my prodigality. Anyway, while the hard-featured saleslady was wrapping them up with appropriate mash notes to each bimbo, I went upstairs to the men's dept. to buy myself a cheap tie-tack. When I returned for the feminine frillies, I found (a) that the saleslady had forgotten to identify which box was which, and (b) that she had switched the notes. In other words, the blonde Amazon would find herself with the brunette's undershirt and some steamy sentiment addressed to the latter, and vice versa. I broke out into a perspiration—it's tropically hot in those department stores anyway—and insisted on the saleslady clawing open the boxes, which meant destroying all the fake holly berries, silver cord, and mishmash they were entwined in. This of course put her in a foul temper, and meanwhile a waiting queue of customers became incensed. The upshot was a group shot of seven or eight people leering and cackling obscenely as I stood there holding the two chemises and the notes appropriate to the recipients. Given the savoir faire of Cary Grant I might have risen above it, but the only savoir faire I possess is Oliver Hardy's, and little enough of that. . . .

When Perelman's letters are collected, as they surely deserve to be, they will comprise the autobiography he promised and began, but never get around to finishing. The three chapters printed here are all we have of *The Hindsight Saga.* Anyway, with a title that good you hardly need a book; or did its promise of disclosures intimidate him? He was always more personal and ruminative and risqué in his letters than he was in his stories, and he heartily disliked people who boasted by reminiscing about the past. "I see Scott Fitzgerald's gossip-columnist mistress has been cleaning out the contents of a thimble," he wrote me when Sheilah Graham's *The Real Scott Fitzgerald* appeared.

Perelman knew Fitzgerald as a sober, hard-working scriptwriter, who had gone to Hollywood for the money, much as today's writers accept tenure at universities. Fitzgerald believed himself a failure, but Perelman was one man (Faulkner was another) who used Hollywood to fuel his other projects; his script-writing career coincided with his first appearance in the pages of *The New Yorker*. It seems extraordinary that he was able to keep his enthusiasms separate, but to California and New York he added the world. From the thirties onward he traveled widely, first in the Pacific and then in Africa, Europe and Asia. I cannot think of another writer who was so adept as Perelman in prevailing over such vast cultural incongruities and whose appreciations included B-movies, pulp magazines, Joyce's *Ulysses*, Hollywood dives, the societal norms in Bucks County, Manhattan and Nairobi, detective fiction, English country-house weekends, vintage cars, dogs (he once, on a whim, bought a bloodhound), cantankerous producers and pretty women. He talked with passionate energy about Fellini's *Satyricon* and Alfred Russel Wallace's *The Malay Archipelago*. He knew Dorothy Parker well and had a close friendship with Eric Ambler. He was the only person I have ever known who dropped in on J. D. Salinger, whom he called "Jerry."

His greatest passion was language. In "Listen to the Mockingbird" he wrote, "As recently as 1918, it was possible for a housewife in Providence, where I grew up, to march into a store with a five-cent piece, purchase a firkin of cocoa butter, a good second-hand copy of Bowditch, a hundredweight of quahogs, a shagreen spectacle case and sufficient nainsook for a corset cover and emerge with enough left over to buy a balcony admission to *The Masquerader* with Guy Bates Post, and a box of maxixe cherries." He was parodying inflation, but it is impossible to read "cocoa butter," "Bowditch," "quahogs," "shagreen," "nainsook," and the rest without a sense of mounting hilarity. He worked hard for a kind of insane exactitude in his prose and would not settle for "sad" if he could use "chopfallen." I think his travels were bound up with his quest to find odd words or possible puns. They were more than mere souvenirs of travel: they were the object of his arduous jaunts. The uniqueness of his writing depends for its effects on linguistic virtuosity, finding room for "oppidan" or the verb "swan" or the weirder lingo he abstracted in India and Africa. E. B. White once wrote about how Perelman, after crashing his car in Florida, savored the phrase "We totaled it!" and how his pleasure in being able to use it took the sting out of the accident.

His interests and his travels swelled his vocabulary and gave him his style. But none of this would have been accessible without his memory, which was faultless. That too is a distinguishing feature in his fiction. A good memory is one of the most valuable assets a writer has, and Perelman's memory amounted to genius. One day, years ago, he was passing through Shropshire, and a glimpse of that green countryside stayed with him. He plotted to return to Shropshire and rent a house and live there like a squire; but though he visited England often, he always became restive. Apart from the precincts of *Punch*, where he was feted, he found England tight and dry and a little dull. And the house rents in Shropshire were too high. He was too much of an Anglophile to like England greatly.

He died on October 17, 1979, in New York City, where he was born. The stories that are collected here previously appeared in *The New Yorker*, but the chapters from *The Hindsight Saga* are being published for the first time. His writing did not flag in fifty years, and this, his twentieth book, is as funny as anything he ever wrote.

PART ONE

"And Then the Whining
Schoolboy, with His Satchel"
and Other Pieces
1974–1979

And Then the Whining
Schoolboy, with His Satchel

At four o'clock of a late-February afternoon in 1919, an icicle four feet long depending from the nose of Sultan Abdul-Hamid II, the potentate whose granite countenance graced the façade of the Turk's Head Building in Providence, cascaded four stories to the sidewalk below, narrowly missing Morris Schreiber, an insurance salesman who was hurrying at that moment to sell Azouf Harootunian, the manager of the Weybosset Market, an accident policy. In the barbershop of the Crown Hotel, simultaneously, Walt Zymchuck, in charge of the second chair, was lathering Edward Gipf, a retired jewelry executive, when, because of the intense cold, the Bakelite handle of his shaving brush broke off and lodged a soapy pellicle of badger hair in his client's throat, occasioning momentary strangulation. Less than twenty minutes later, the accumulation of frozen snow on the roof of Cherry & Webb's specialty shop on Westminster Street caused a skylight to buckle in such wise that icy drafts whipped down an interior wall. A family of mice domiciled there scampered into the corset department, and in the resultant stampede Mrs. Anna Rubashkin of Central Falls suffered a number of contusions from splintered whalebone.

While these and similar human-interest stories were breaking all over Providence in what was inevitably described as the

19

worst freeze in weather annals, another event, far more epochal from my point of view, was about to occur in the city. On Exchange Place, the municipal mall dominated by an equestrian statue of General Ambrose Burnside, stood a popular tearoom and soda fountain—an Elysian temple of goodies which, to avoid any imputation that it was run by Greeks, bore the prosaic name of Gibson's. So seductive was the ambrosial smell of its cakes, pies, cookies, twists, and rings, its chocolates, caramels, mints, and nougats, and the syrups and garnishes employed in its parfaits, smashes, cabinets, and banana splits that travellers had been known to leap from trains passing through the Union Station, three blocks away, and squander their patrimony there with no thought for the morrow. Five or six years earlier, indeed, a stockroom clerk at the Pussy Willow Ruching Corporation, famed throughout New England for feminine neckwear, had embezzled a quantity of jabots, altered the labels on their boxes, and sold them to unsuspecting French Canadians as sabots. Since the offender had spent the entire proceeds on brownies, éclairs, and macaroons at Gibson's and lapsed into a state of coma, the judge, a compassionate man with a sweet tooth, tempered justice with mercy and remitted the sentence.

It was to the foregoing establishment, then, that I had been invited that afternoon for a rendezvous with a lady a dozen years my senior—a situation that, considering I was a raw youth, might suggest the sort of liaison popularized by Colette or Arthur Schnitzler. Actually, the inception of the meeting was quite innocent. Just as our sophomore English class at high school was dispersing that morning, the teacher, Miss Cronjager, summoned me to her desk. Over the weekend, it emerged, she had been grading some compositions of an autobiographical nature submitted by the class, and she felt that mine needed clarification. "I was originally going to discuss it with you in my office," she said, "but on second thought it might be better if we did so in a less constrained atmosphere. I have an errand or two not far from Gibson's, so let's you and I meet there for a nice cup of tea and a chat."

Inasmuch as Miss Cronjager had honey-colored hair and a figure evocative of the coryphées portrayed in cigarette pictures, I saw no reason to gag at the proposal and turned up well ahead of time. Before long, I began salivating as waitresses ran to and fro bearing charlotte russes, schnecken, and gooseberry tarts to the women shoppers about me; at last, tortured by the rich aroma of hot chocolate and spicy fruitcake, my will power collapsed, and I ordered a portion of jelly roll and a coffee float. The question of payment for the snack did not concern me. After all, I reasoned, since Miss Cronjager had initiated the conference, it was her obligation to pick up the tab.

Half an hour passed without any sign of Miss Cronjager, and, fearful that the management might deem me a stiff loitering in the premises to keep warm, I ordered a butterscotch ice-cream soda and a slice of angel cake topped with hazelnuts and chocolate sauce. What with the surrounding turbulence, I succeeded in remaining persona grata for another thirty minutes, but then panic overtook me. My repast thus far totalled one dollar and eighty-five cents, and all I had on me was my carfare home. Fantasies began multiplying wherein Miss Cronjager had broken an ankle en route or been run down by a streetcar. The consequences—a hullabaloo of exposure, arrest, arraignment in juvenile court—were too horrid to contemplate. Moreover, and as if to intensify my qualms, a busboy materialized and polished the table to a high gloss while the manager, arms folded behind his cash register, surveyed me menacingly.

Luckily, before I could throw myself at his feet and plead for mercy, Miss Cronjager appeared, flushed and rosy from the biting cold. She was wearing a Russian pony coat, and every woman in the place immediately turned sick with hatred.

"I hope I haven't kept you waiting," she apologized. "You should have had something to eat." I mumbled some gallantry of a Spartan nature, which she brushed aside. "No, no—order some cinnamon toast or buns, whatever you'd like. I'll just have tea." Feigning elaborate reluctance, I studied the menu, torn between mocha layer cake and a walnut sundae with ladyfingers.

Rather than be categorized as a glutton, however, I checked myself and settled for an eight-inch segment of poppy-seed strudel and a vanilla freeze.

"Now, then," Miss Cronjager began, as lethargy from an excess of carbohydrates stole over me, "very likely, you wonder why I chose to hold our discussion here instead of at school. The reason is that the essay you wrote about your past . . ." She hesitated. "Well, it raised some personal questions that I felt could be better answered in a heart-to-heart talk."

My pulse skipped a beat, a hot blush rose to the roots of my hair, and a mixture of anxiety and guilt churned in my breast. Had I willingly divulged some dark corner of my psyche, visible only to an adult? Had Miss Cronjager, reading between the lines, sensed with her feminine intuition the fantasies I sometimes cherished about her, particularly before falling asleep?

"Eh—sure, Miss Cronjager," I said. "What would you like to know?"

She reached under her chair and withdrew my theme from her briefcase. "Well, let's go over it in detail. Your earliest boyhood memory, you say, was of a village on the rocky, fogbound coast of Maine, of rough but kindly fishermen hauling lobster pots and mending their nets. Occasionally, when they voyaged to the Grand Banks in their schooners, they took you along, because you recall men in dories detaching codfish from hand lines. Now, on one of these voyages you made the acquaintance of an English lad, who had accidentally fallen off a transatlantic liner and been rescued by your vessel, with whom you became fast friends. Tell me"—she broke off—"did you ever read a book by Rudyard Kipling called *Captains Courageous?*"

"Not that I remember," I said. "Why?"

"Oh, I was just curious," she said. "One other point. Not far from the village, you state, there was an isolated tavern named the Admiral Benbow Inn, frequented by suspicious characters who clinked gold coins when they roistered and sang nautical chanteys. Together with the boy whose mother ran the tavern—his name, you believe, was Hawkins—you hid in an apple barrel and ascertained that these men were mutineers. How large was this barrel that it could accommodate two boys?"

"It was more of a keg—a hogshead, like, with iron hoops," I explained. "They used them for rum and molasses, too. The inside was real sticky."

" 'Sticky' is a good description," agreed Miss Cronjager. "I felt that when I read the passage. All right, we come next to the stage in your narrative where your folks have moved to a cotton plantation in Dixie. Your account of their huge pillared mansion, with a family retainer named Uncle Cudgo, Southern belles waltzing with their escorts, and field hands strumming banjos, is very colorful, but you neglect to mention where the money for all this came from. I was under the impression that your parents' livelihood derived from catching finny denizens."

"It came about through a legacy, I believe," I said. "I remember a lawyer bringing us some stocks and bonds in a hamper, but I was too young to understand."

"Besides, you were rebellious," she reminded me. "As you point out, you soon tired of all the fussing, the endless coddling of nurses and tutors, and you ran away to the Texas Panhandle, to live the life of a cowboy. You must have been the youngest cowhand in the West at that time."

I nodded. "I was, but if you read *Riders of the Purple Sage* or *The Winning of Barbara Worth*, there were lots of young fellows seeking their fortunes out there. I mean, it was the frontier, and it took plenty of vim to rope and tie the dogies, brand the mavericks, and stave off attacks of the marauding red man."

"From which you didn't flinch one iota, I'm sure," she said warmly. "Was that how you became a rustler?"

"A rustler?" I repeated. "Not a rustler, Miss Cronjager—a *wrestler*. You see, the family objected to my life on the range and packed me off to Lawrenceville, where I made the varsity team and hung around with ginks like your Doc Macnooder, the Tennessee Shad, and so forth."

"What a privilege to have known those fabled characters of Owen Johnson's personally, rather than through the printed page like the rest of us," she observed enviously. "However, at that juncture, I confess, I was mystified. Why didn't you go on to Yale thereafter?"

"Gee, I thought I made that clear," I said. "Dink Stover was the big man on campus there, and I was afraid that our rivalry —well, I hate to say it . . ."

"No, go on," she urged. "You're much too self-effacing."

"I felt there wasn't room for us both," I said. "And, besides, I had those two projects I couldn't decide between."

"Oh, yes, I forgot." She consulted my pages. "Whether to track down the insidious Dr. Fu Manchu or to join Allan Quatermain in the Mountains of the Moon. You really were on the horns of a dilemma, weren't you?"

"Worse than that," I said. "The Yukon was calling, too, and the South Seas. One minute, I saw myself skimming over the frozen wastes in a dogsled driven by some laconic sourdough; the next, I was piloting a longboat manned by seven bronzed Kanakas through the surf at Rarotonga."

"Now, that's the part of your reminiscences that puzzled me most," said Miss Cronjager. "With all these clashing impulses, what finally brought you back to Providence and the Classical High School? For one whose history is so colorful, don't you find existence here a bit prosaic—humdrum, in fact?"

"Well, it's not as exciting as some places," I admitted. "I remember one time when I was a supercargo aboard a Swedish tramp bound from Mombasa to Tientsin. It was typhoon weather in the South China Sea, and we were scudding along under bare poles—"

"Wait a minute," she interrupted. "When did this take place? There's no indication here that you ever shipped before the mast."

"Look, Miss Cronjager," I expostulated. "When you assigned us this subject, you said to make it brief—to just emphasize the salient points. If I put down all the adventures I've had, it would read like *The Arabian Nights' Entertainments.*"

"It does even now," she said. "That in a way is what I'm driving at. Tell me, how old are you?"

I replied that I had recently celebrated my fifteenth birthday.

"Well, you certainly have led a life jam-packed with incident. And," she added, with an enigmatic smile, "you've managed to squeeze in quite a lot of reading, haven't you?"

Stupefied though I was by my sugar intake, some instinct warned me at that moment that the question was loaded, and in a flash the truth dawned on me. In my innocence, I had accepted the teacher–pupil relationship at face value, only to fall victim to the third degree. Miss Cronjager, for all her silken benevolence, sought to trap me into admitting that my past was a tissue of falsehoods—a collage, or mosaic, of the great books that had enriched my youth. Instantly, I was on the qui vive. In the next breath, this woman might very well demolish me with charges of plagiarism, forever ruin my credibility. Luckily, if the hours I had spent with Leatherstocking, with Sax Rohmer's Nayland Smith, and with Craig Kennedy, the Scientific Detective, had taught me nothing else, they had honed my sense of caution to razor sharpness. I had learned that destruction lurked behind the snap of a twig in the forest path, that a trifling cigarette ash could doom even the most cunning individual and bring his house of cards crashing down on his head. It may seem incredible that a mere fifteen-year-old should be capable of so complex a chain of reasoning, yet it hurtled through my mind with the speed of an express train, and in the next instant my foil parried Miss Cronjager's thrust with lightning swordsmanship.

"Why, yes," I returned, my lips curving in the exact Oriental smile that Sydney Greenstreet was to popularize several decades later. "I occasionally like to while away the idle hour with a book, as who does not? However," I went on, rising, "I fear I detain you. If you have no further questions, Miss Cronjager, it is incumbent on me to scoot. The Y.M.C.A. gymnastics team, which I captain, is competing tonight for the Horace Dooley silver cup, and I must insure that everything in the way of sweatshirts and similar gear is in apple-pie order."

Had Miss Cronjager known that far from being captain, or even a member, of any gymnastics team, I could not vault over a sawhorse without sustaining multiple fractures, I would not have escaped so easily. For whatever reason, though—possibly out of sheer ennui—she interposed no objection, and I beat a hasty retreat. Several days later, I was chopfallen to discover that I had received a mark of D-minus for my handiwork. To this day, I can think of no adequate explanation. Perhaps, aggrieved by the staggering bill she paid at Gibson's, Miss Cronjager revenged herself by flunking me—a disheartening instance of the Dickensian cruelty prevalent at that time in New England high schools. Nonetheless, and by what rare gifts of forbearance in my makeup I cannot say, I never bore her a grudge. Maybe it was that stern upbringing in the Maine fisheries, mellowed by plantation life in the old South and matured at Lawrenceville and in the South Seas, that made me incapable of vindictiveness. Or maybe it was that honey-colored hair and exquisite figure I still remember, particularly before falling asleep. *¿Quién sabe?*

One of Our Stagecraft Is Missing

In these days when rock stars hatch one evening and perish the next with the mortality of mayflies, how many of those who, like myself, idolized him ever give a thought to Liberace? All of us were spellbound by his meteoric rise, hungrily followed his career, and kept his picture under our pillow, but I suppose that essentially we looked upon him as a great, gorgeous peacock who shed enchantment on our lives and then flapped off into obscurity. So it was a signal for rejoicing when the night-club page of *Variety* blossomed forth recently with a review of his new act at the Las Vegas Hilton, the essence of which was that he had once more breathtakingly demonstrated his virtuosity. Said the account, "Liberace outdoes himself on each return with a more spectacular wardrobe (this time it's a dazzler whipped up by young designer Jim Lapidus), more expensive automobiles to deliver him onstage, more colorful supporting acts (the Little Angels of Korea are aboard currently), and more surprises. The surprise this trip is not his entrance, which is surprising enough, but his exit—he literally flies off the stage and into the wings suspended by wire à la Peter Pan. It adds up to a fine funfest bursting with extra flair by the master showman."

My initial reaction, understandably, was one of awe; it must have taken an engineering genius like Isambard Kingdom Brunel, the wizard who built the Great Eastern, to whisk someone of Liberace's girth into limbo before the audience's eyes.

27

Yet that was only half the problem; after he described his parabola, how had they cushioned his descent? Was he pitchforked onto a hair mattress or feather bed, a firemen's net stretched by half a dozen stagehands? The report cast no light on such technicalities, and perhaps it was just as well. Coruscating and effulgent in his jewelled finery, Liberace had again flashed across the firmament like Halley's comet, creating a moment of theatrical magic. To equivocate about the phenomenon would be as idle as analyzing a moonbeam.

Keen though my pleasure was at Liberace's resurgence, I was nagged by a feeling that somewhere in the past I, too, had assisted in the lightning disappearance of an actor. It couldn't have been connected with *Peter Pan*, since I never saw Barrie's play and my only association with him was that pipe smoker's bible, *My Lady Nicotine*, in some freshman dormitory when heated disputes raged about the relative merits of Barking Dog and Imperial Cube Cut and people used to rub Dunhill briars along the side of their nose to bring out the beauty of the grain. No, my imbroglio had some reference to show business, but stap my vitals if I could pin it down. Just as I was chastising myself for an amnesic old pantaloon, a chance encounter provided the clue that resurrected the whole thing.

I was combing the kitchenware section of Macy's for a prosaic enough appliance—an hourglass gauging how long to boil an egg. All I could find was a Swiss monstrosity (a tiny glass cathedral filled with blue plastic beads) and a nine-dollar automatic timer that switched on lights to deceive burglars. The salesgirl, a Mexican Indian from Mazatlán who had not had my advantages, was unable to grasp what I sought.

"An hourglass," I pleaded, sculpturing a figure in the air like Lillian Russell's. "You know, the same on top as on the bottom. . . . For boiling *huevos*—like the one Father Time carries with his scythe."

Irked by her utter incomprehension, I threw up my hands and flung off, nearly capsizing a middle-aged woman burdened with shopping bags. Before I could apologize, her face brightened. "Why, hello, stranger!" she said, chortling. "Don't you remember me? I'm Noreen Cannister—have you forgotten? I played Gloria Kramer in *One Touch of Venus*."

Well, her features evoked no memory of any in the cast I treasured, but after a struggle I succeeded in placing her. Her married name was Breastbohn, she disclosed, and her husband had an automobile agency in Plainfield, New Jersey.

"Now, promise me," she urged as we parted. "If you ever should pass through Plainfield—"

I pledged I would stop by for the clam fritters or shoofly pie or whatever delicacy Plainfield was renowned for, and left. Almost an hour later, the full significance of our meeting hit me. But of course! This was the party—this selfsame Noreen Cannister—whose inexplicable fate I had been groping to recover from the past.

In the autumn of 1943, the company of *One Touch of Venus* was in New York, girding itself for its Boston tryout under the direction of Elia Kazan. The libretto Ogden Nash and I had fashioned for Kurt Weill's score was an intricate one, but, stripped of its details, as it was by Kazan doggedly, it concerned the goddess's infatuation with a barber. One of the key scenes dealt with a quarrel in the latter's shop between his fiancée, Gloria, and Venus, at the climax of which the incensed divinity, with an imperious gesture, caused her rival to disappear on the spot.

"That may take a little doing," observed Kazan, who had had some small experience in amateur theatricals.

Luckily, we had foreseen his objection. There was, said Nash, a person named Cubbage, a member of the Society of American Magicians expert in such illusions, who had signified his readiness to tackle the problem if a proper quid pro quo was forthcoming. Skeptical at first that anyone could be made to evaporate in full light, Kazan finally agreed to run the scene for the magician. Cubbage, a lanky stringbean of a man resembling Pee Wee Russell, watched the action, pondered awhile, and assured us he could work it out.

"That's what we call a mid-stage vanish," he explained. Then scrutinizing Gloria, he asked, "Tell me—do you have to use that actress again?" Kazan replied that she was indispensable, and Cubbage sighed. "It's a shame," he said. "I could have given you a really spectacular trick. Anyhow, don't worry. I'll get back to you. I have to measure a few barber chairs for what I have in mind."

The solution he returned with was brilliant in its simplicity. A conventional barber chair would be altered in but one respect —its back to consist of a hollow replica five inches deeper than the original, masked by a roller curtain of simulated leather. During the altercation, Venus would advance on Gloria with arm upraised so that the girl staggered backward into the seat, drawing up her knees in terror. As the goddess majestically consigned her to oblivion, the chair would begin revolving. Gloria would jackknife into its hollow in her fetal position, and within two and a half quick revolutions she would effectively vanish into thin air.

Despite managerial outcries at the expense of Cubbage's device and forebodings from Kazan that Gloria might suffocate inside it, majority opinion hailed the idea as sensational. Word was dispatched to the scenic studio to ready the chair for the Boston tryout, now less than a fortnight distant. In the attendant frenzy of preparation, none of us alluded to the subject again; while the fate of the show was unpredictable, Gloria's mid-stage vanish was a cinch. We could already hear the cheers of the opening-night audience as it gave the scene a standing ovation.

At the dress rehearsal in Boston's Colonial Theatre, costumes ripped, scenery buckled, and tempers frazzled, but the illusion worked superbly. The two principals and the chair performed with brio, spiriting away Gloria like a puff of smoke. There was only one imperfection—a drawback, to put it mildly, that no-body could have anticipated. On Gloria's scheduled reappearance in the plot, she failed to turn up on cue. The rehearsal ground to a stop as emissaries scouted dressing rooms, the lounges, adjacent lunchrooms in vain. Saddled with a vast company of mummers, dancers, singers, and musicians frozen into inactivity, not to mention nineteen stagehands drawing overtime pay, Kazan tore out handfuls of hair—an action that threatened to leave him as bald as an egg. But the search was unavailing; by whatever agency, human or divine, the girl had in fact disappeared and divil a bit if anyone had seen her go.

At the première the following night, Gloria's understudy took over the role, playing the scene without the use of Cubbage's prop. Instead, Venus wrought her magic on a stage aquiver with thunder and lightning, and the girl stole off through the murk. The audience, inured to displays of thunder and lightning, failed to respond with a standing ovation. Nash and I, draped over the orchestra rail, were embittered by the thought of what might have been. To further lacerate our self-esteem, Kazan, whenever he beheld the two of us thereafter, would sardonically comment, "There go Cubbage and Burbage."

It followed as the night the day, hence, that, having collided with Noreen Cannister, I was avid to quiz the lady about her untimely disappearance, and I hastened to phone her. However, since I had stupidly forgotten her married name of Breastbohn, this presented a difficulty; I remembered it as something like Sternum or Midriff, but no such person was listed in Plainfield. Ultimately, I sequestered her through her husband's car lot, and we met for lunch in an Italian restaurant in the Village whose ambience I felt would encourage confidences. She was, as I expected, reluctant at the outset to yield up particulars, but three Side Cars and a quantity of Verdicchio loosened her tongue. It was a bizarre story.

Six months before joining our musical, Noreen had met a wealthy furrier named, if I recall, Max Bibulous, who fell madly in love with her. She described him as magnetic rather than handsome, adding that, though overweight, squat, and brusque, he radiated a sense of power. He was also the soul of generosity; he lavished jewels and clothes and flowers on her without stint and sought to install her in a Park Avenue garçonnière, which she found unacceptable. He, on his part, drew the line at marriage, claiming that his insanely jealous wife would drink iodine if he left her. Their friendship grew ever more tempestuous as his ardor increased, and on the eve of her departure for Boston he proposed that they run away to Brazil and start life anew. She derided the idea, a fierce quarrel ensued, and the evening ended with her vow never to see him again.

To boil down her rather diffuse narrative, she recalled that on the night of the dress rehearsal she felt giddy after her spin in the barber chair and had gone out the stage door for a breath of air. In the alley, she was accosted by a burly individual—a sailor, seemingly, for he had on a peajacket—who said that Bibulous, in a limousine outside, wished to speak to her. Foolishly unsuspecting, she started toward the curb, suddenly felt herself overpowered and smothered by a cloth exuding some noxious liquid, and knew no more. When she regained consciousness, she was in a hopeless predicament—a prisoner aboard a yacht, chartered by Bibulous, steaming for Brazil. So overcome was she by rage at his perfidy, by agitation at the ruin of her career, that her sanity almost gave way. No amount of supplication or of appeals to his finer nature produced the slightest effect; he countered with word pictures of their future together on vast *estancias*, of the carnival gaiety of Rio and journeys up the Amazon. Drained of emotion, corroded with bitterness, she locked herself in her cabin, resolved to starve herself to death.

"I don't know how long I was in there," she went on tragically. "I was so weak that time ceased to exist for me. Then the boat stopped moving, and in my delirium I thought we were in Rio, till Max forced the door and told me."

"Where were you?"

"In Camden, New Jersey. Max was crying and blubbering like a little boy. His whole world was in pieces. He had just been handed a cable by the harbor master—I forgot his name—"

"Never mind his name," I interrupted. "What was in the cable?"

"It was from his accountant, Irving Previne. It said that his wife and his partner had cheated him out of his share in the business and eloped together. He didn't have a dime—only enough to pay the mooring fee. He begged me not to desert him —he was going to open a small fur shop in Mount Holly and begin over again if I would stick by him."

"But you were free," I objected. "Why didn't you come back to the show?"

"What, and be cooped up in that chair eight times a week?" she scoffed. "Listen, I was a nervous wreck, but I had some sense left. I hitchhiked as far as Plainfield, where luck smiled on me and I ran into Nels Breastbohn. Today, I have three darling kiddies, a devoted husband, and a lovely ranch-style home. So I guess I should be grateful."

Especially, I thought, to a man named Cubbage, who was more of a magician than he knew. "Still and all," I said, "don't you sometimes miss the glamour of show business?"

"Oh, *that*." She shrugged. "I can get all of that I need from a copy of *Variety*."

Which, considering what that journal's review of Liberace had done for me, took the words right out of my mouth.

The Frost Is on the Noggin

I once asked the retired fly cop Dashiell Hammett, a former Pinkerton employee who'd switched to writing for the pulps, a technical question about surveillance. In his experience as a sleuth, I inquired, was a person under suspicion ever conscious of being shadowed? Hammett responded with an anecdote. It seems that a certain New York jewelry concern had a drummer named Finsterwald—a Teutonicism for "Darkwood"—whose honesty it had reason to question. Finsterwald was about to go South on a sales trip, bearing two cases of valuable samples the firm believed he was planning to steal, and Hammett was detailed to keep an eye on him. Conspicuous for his height, emaciation, and snow-white thatch, Hammett was an unlikely choice for the job, but, as it happened, all the other operatives were out breaking strikes or retrieving gold falcons or whatever gumshoes of that era busied themselves with.

Finsterwald, closely followed by Hammett, entrained for Philadelphia and on arrival there checked into a hotel. Hammett got a room two doors away, ate dinner at an adjacent table in the coffee shop, and yawned in concert with him in the lobby until bedtime. The next morning, the salesman took off for Hagerstown, where he and his shadow went through the same uneventful routine. In the ensuing five days, the pair progressed in succession to Richmond, Raleigh, Knoxville, Columbia, and Macon. Nowhere in his zigzag pattern was Finsterwald ever out of Hammett's sight for a moment during waking hours, nor did he call on a single prospect. His manner was unhurried and devoid of the slightest hint of furtiveness. Not once by word or deed did he exhibit any awareness that he was under scrutiny.

Midafternoon on the eighth day of the trip, according to Hammett, he was sitting in a park in Savannah, idling through a newspaper and observing Finsterwald as the latter dozed on a bench nearby. Distracted by some item of unusual interest in the paper, he forgot his quarry for an instant. Suddenly a voice sounded at his elbow. Finsterwald, a diffident smile on his face, was addressing him.

"Excuse me, but you look familiar. Haven't I seen you somewhere before?"

"Why, no—not that I recall," Hammett returned blandly.

"Strange," mused the salesman. "Oh, well, probably a resemblance . . . Mind if I sit down here?"

Hammett bade him do so, exchanged profundities about the beauty of Savannah, and, upon mutual agreement that its climate, while balmy, aroused thirst, accompanied him to a tavern. After several beers, Finsterwald began oozing bonhomie. He deemed Hammett a capital fellow, one who knew a hawk from a handsaw and could be relied on in a pinch. It was only a guess, but he felt intuitively that his companion might not be averse to making a little easy moola. Affirming that his pores were ever open for a proposition, Hammett asked what he had in mind. The drummer thereupon unfolded a complex scheme that involved stowing the jewelry samples in a Miami railroad checkroom and mailing the claim tickets to Hammett, who would convey the cases to a fence in Zanesville and rendezvous with him in Altoona to split the swag. Amid much cackling, the bargain was sealed over a couple of boilermakers, and they parted—Finsterwald to visit a Turkish bath and Hammett to turn him in at the nearest police station for conspiring to commit larceny.

"And if I know what goes on in stir," Hammett concluded, "that bird spent the next couple of years scratching his head and saying to himself, 'Jeez, it was foolproof—how did they ever catch on? What did I do wrong?' "

Any likelihood that I was about to be drawn into a similarly bizarre situation was farthest from my mind when, several weeks ago, I read a striking report in the London *Times*. "The West Germans are rapidly becoming a nation of shoplifters," it said. "One prosperous businessman stole, over a long period, all the food he wanted for a party he was giving. A titled woman, wearing a fur coat worth thousands of marks, was found to have the lining stuffed full of stolen food. . . . One man shopper took a fancy to a frozen chicken, and went to the extraordinary length of concealing it in the crown of his hat. He was detected at the cash desk, but only because he fell unconscious while waiting to pay for those goods he had decided to declare. The frozen fowl nesting on top of his head had slowed down the blood circulation to his brain."

Not long after I read the foregoing, I happened to notice in the Third Avenue supermarket where I shop a remarkable person contemplating the showcase of frozen foods. Gaunt, well over six feet tall, and chin-whiskered, he was clad in a rusty Prince Albert set off by a silk hat of the type known as a tile. Whether it was his expression of deep melancholy or his posture as he stood grasping his lapels, he reminded me of someone, but I could not remember who. Clearly oblivious of my gaze, he opened the showcase door and withdrew two packages—a Stouffer's beef pie and a Sara Lee cheesecake. At that juncture, some old gaffer maneuvering his wagon jostled me. I stepped aside with an apology, and when I turned back the tall stranger had vanished into the detergents and soap powders. I assumed I had seen the last of him, but no—on reaching the express checkout lane I beheld him directly ahead. The clerk was bagging his sole purchase, a Teflon scouring pad, and, mystified, I watched him exit through the automatic doors. Where were the foodstuffs he'd selected, the beef pie and cheesecake? And who in tarnation was he? There was an enigmatic quality about the man, an elusiveness, apart from his identity, that unsettled me.

Had I consulted my astrological forecast, as I should have, it would have told me I was entering a period of suspense, which

shortly became apparent. Three days thence, the counterman
of a delicatessen on Nineteenth Street was slicing a quarter of
Novy for me. The ambient air was heavy with the fragrance of
whitefish, Maatjes herring, and freshly minted bagels, and,
crowded around me, a bevy of dynamite chicks, each lovelier
than Faye Dunaway, awaited their turn with nostrils flaring.
All of a sudden, like a chill wind, I felt an alien presence, and
there stood the same wraithlike figure by the frozen-food locker,
clasping an icy carton of wonton soup atop two packets of
Chinese snow peas and water chestnuts. I stared at him for what
must have seemed an eternity, because the counterman loosed
an enraged bellow.

"What next, Mister, what next?" the counterman cried.
"People are waiting!"

"Yes, and they're famished!" echoed one of the beauties.
"What's eating you, chum? You look like you seen a ghost."

She was right, in a sense, for in that instant I had witnessed
an uncanny sleight-of-hand performance—the disappearance of
all three eatables into the man's uplifted hat. By the time I
squirmed through the press, clutching my Novy, his only visible
selection, a bar of halvah, had been rung up on the register and
he was speeding down the block. Burning to ascertain whether
the refrigeration would fell him as it had the kraut shoplifter,
I took off in hot pursuit. Our contest was unequal; the gelid ice
cap seemed to act on him like adrenaline, though possibly
he may have raised his sugar level with the halvah. Whatever the
cause, I lost him somewhere near Gramercy Park, but the chase
was not wholly unproductive. In one of several buildings where
he could have gone to earth, I found a mailbox reading Eban
Locnil. It didn't promise much at first, but, thanks to a pipeful
or two of Latakia and an aptitude for cryptography, it re-
arranged itself into Abe Lincoln, and I knew a moment of
elation. So that was why the chap had seemed familiar. Well, I
resolved grimly, *ruat caelum*, I was going to discover how this
dishonest Abe had flouted the most elementary laws of
physiology.

The opportunity came that Saturday, in the hurly-burly of

weekend shopping. Poring through the bins of Nussbaum's Gourmeteria, on Second Avenue, for a breakfast kipper, I overheard a woman railing against the rudeness of a customer who, she asserted, had practically wrenched a broiler out of her hand. "He's some kind of a poultry freak, the muzzler!" she shrilled. "He's there right now at the meat counter! An old-fashioned weirdo in a high hat."

Sparse though it was, her description warranted a rundown, and I tiptoed into the next aisle. The sight that met my eyes was well-nigh past belief. Disdaining easy choices like goose liver and chicken wings, my Presidential doppelgänger was about to execute a *coup de théâtre* by forcing a butterball turkey into his headpiece. Providentially, he did not see me, and I ducked back. That was all to the good. If there was to be a confrontation, I wanted it on my own terms.

"Reach for the sky, Locnil." The words I had rehearsed since quitting Nussbaum's sounded less puissant at the entrance of his brownstone, but they gained menace from the briar pipe I jammed into his back. He stiffened, and before he could resist I herded him into the foyer. Then I did some quick thinking. If he lamped a Dunhill in my mitt instead of a police special, the jig was up, so I shifted it to my coat pocket. I wasn't sure if he'd buy it, but he bought it. All the way up in the poky little elevator, he spoke only once.

"You the fuzz?"

"Uh-uh, just someone who knows his way around the circulatory system and needs a few answers. This your pad?"

He nodded, fiddled with the locks, threw on a switch. Then, as the room flooded with light, he swung around, his eyes twin clouded agates. "All right, what's bugging you?" he snarled. "Talk fast. I've got a turkey melting on my head."

"Boohoo, you're breaking my heart," I growled. "Sit down, Lincoln, and keep your hands on your lapels. That way nobody gets hurt."

His face fell apart. "How did you know me?"

"I wasn't born yesterday. Anyway, there aren't too many gees around that look like rail-splitters. Once I ruled out Raymond

Massey and Arthur Miller, there was only one other person you could be."

"Listen, you," he said, his twin agates narrowing. "I got a hunch you've been tailing me. I'm positive we've seen each other in the past."

"Maybe you were a king in Babylon and I was a Christian slave," I chaffed him. "But enough with the yocks. Where did you get the idea?"

"I don't read you. What idea?"

"Of wearing a heated wig on your sconce for insulation—to counteract the deadly frost that you knew would cause syncope, from cerebral anemia."

He figured the odds a long moment, decided I had him. "You win, Doc," he said. "But how did you tumble? Tell me where I goofed."

"For one thing, at the meat counter in Nussbaum's. You stepped out of character, my friend. The Great Emancipator would never have snatched a broiler from a lady."

"Yeah, I guess I overplayed my hand. What else?"

I flicked aside his muffler, exposing the electric cord leading under his hat. "At first, I thought you had a can of Sterno up there, or a small hibachi. Then I spotted this when you were heisting the gobbler. That cinched it, Locnil."

Rarely have I seen such desolation on a human countenance; staring out at me, all pretense flown, was a mute hunted animal. He silently extended his wrists. "O.K., I'm ready. Let's go."

I extracted my pipe, tapped out the dottle, and rose. "Smarten up, fellow," I said. "I told you—I'm not a lawman. Nor am I, in spite of your awed expression, that implausible creation of Jacques Futrelle's, The Thinking Machine."

"Then who are you, in God's name?" he whimpered.

"Merely an insomniac," I said. "A reader of the London Times who can't rest until he solves their news reports." And went out the door.

Zwei Herzen in die Drygoods Schlock

"Everyone else is talking about me," said Diane Von Furstenberg, the 29-year-old princess turned dress designer whose fashion empire grossed $60 million last year. "So I figured, why don't I?"

Not content with just being one of the most successful designers to make waves in the recession/inflation fashion economy, Miss Von Furstenberg has now set her heart on literary acclaim. Her next project is a book. It will hit the stores in September and will be titled "Beauty" . . .

"I'm not beautiful—I'm interesting looking. But I've done a lot of work on accepting myself. . . . I've never been a designer," she says. "I was just a woman who walked into her closet one day and realized that everything was out of date."

Ron Talsky, 41, the Hollywood costume designer whose main claim to fashion fame has been designing for Raquel Welch, says they've split.

"I no longer want to be considered by Hollywood as Raquel Welch's designer," says Talsky, who is Oscar-nominated this year for his Welch wardrobe in "The Four Musketeers."

It's not sour grapes. "I'm proud of changing Raquel's image from a young sexpot to a sexy actress," says Talsky, "but I'd like to work with Streisand, Faye Dunaway, Candice Bergen now."   —*Los Angeles Times*

SCENE: *A closet in Los Angeles. As the curtain rises, Charisma von Ausgespielt, a breathtakingly beautiful twenty-four-year-old woman no longer in the first bloom of youth, stands before the door, racked with indecision. After a moment, the door opens and a young man emerges.*

CHARISMA (*startled*): Mercy! Who are you?

40

MAN: What do you mean who am I? Can't you see? I'm a person who's just come out of the closet.

CHARISMA: I realize that, but it still doesn't explain what you were doing in there.

MAN: That's between me and my shrink, nosy. I don't feel obliged to account for my life style to every Tom, Dick, and Harry. (*He exits.*)

CHARISMA: My goodness, what a pepper pot. You can't hardly rummage through your own schmottas nowadays without some ignatz snaps your head off. (*She enters closet and begins sorting dresses, disillusion writ large on her countenance.*) Ugh, to think I ever wore such anachronistic frocks—I must have seemed a frump indeed in these habiliments. However, thanks to a clever needle and the shrewd midwifery of *Women's Wear Daily, Burke's Peerage,* and the *Almanach de Gotha,* I am now on easy street, a biggie in the garment center, and almost finished scrivening my forthcoming smash autobio, *She Spins to Conquer.*

(*Unbeknownst to her, Ricky Tickitavsky, a divinely handsome Hollywood designer, has entered the closet. He is twenty-seven, soigné, and Oscar-rejected for his inept costuming of Anatole France's Jocasta and the Famished Cat.*)

RICKY: Excuse me, Miss—can you tell me the price of these rejects?

CHARISMA (*confounded*): Eek! Where did you come from?

RICKY: Well, it's a long story. My father was born in Lithuania—

CHARISMA: I daresay. Nevertheless, that hardly entitles you to march in here as bold as brass.

RICKY: I don't get you. This is a thrift shop, isn't it? Look at all the schmottas on the rack.

CHARISMA (*icily*): I'll have you know these are all Charisma von Ausgespielt originals.

RICKY: Right, and they've got just the tacky, old-fashioned

quality I need. I'm costuming a revival of *Charley's Aunt* at the Pasadena Senior High School.

CHARISMA: Young man, do you know who you're talking to? I'm the designer of these gowns.

RICKY: So what? I'm a designer, too—Ricky Tickitavsky. You probably read about me in the newspapers.

CHARISMA: Yes, I seem to recall something to the effect that you had just split with Sally Rand.

RICKY: Not Sally Rand—Talleyrand. I changed his image from a sexy young statesman to a sexy older statesman, but it didn't fulfill me. Now I'm thirsting to work with Metternich, Lord Rosebery, Kissinger—the power élite.

CHARISMA: Of course, of course. You mean you want to burst forth from your pupa.

RICKY: What pupa is that?

CHARISMA: Why, your chrysalis—that dull husk which it has heretofore imprisoned your personality. You want to soar out on great golden butterfly wings, to express your potential, to dazzle the onlookers.

RICKY: You know something? You have a way with words. Given the right training, you could be a terrific salesman.

CHARISMA: I sense that in you, too—you have a flair for verbs. Bugging you, though, is the one hurdle: can you accept yourself?

RICKY: (*miserably*): I hate myself. I'm only a—what did you call me before?—a pupa. Sometimes, laying awake in my lonely condominium in Brentwood, I ask myself what behooves it that Vidal Sassoon styles my hair and Yves Saint Laurent makes my cologne, that I drive an Audi Fox. My whole ego is in shards. I feel I'm, like, living a lie.

CHARISMA: *Selbstverständlich*—that's because in your heart's deep core you know yourself to be a pushcart peddler. Now, I was born to the purple, sprung from the proudest loins in Europe, so I don't have these hangups.

RICKY: Forgive me, Highness, but could we sit down maybe? It's kind of close in here.

CHARISMA (*wounded*): Well, after all, it *is* a closet.

RICKY: I'm not criticizing it—I just thought we'd be more comfortable on these shoeboxes. . . . There, that's better. You were saying you sprang from a pride of loins?

CHARISMA: Yes, I mingle with crowned heads as naturally as a duck takes to water, like a baby loves its rock-and-rye. Is there a pheasant drive across the Tweed, a boar hunt in Styria, a gala at Bad Ischl, a champagne party aboard a dahabeah on the Nile? Wherever the *jeunesse dorée* convokes, wherever fun is at its maddest, look for me there, the cynosure of all the men, the envy of all the women. Tell me—do you find me attractive?

RICKY: No, you have something that transcends mere beauty. You have flaring nostrils like a horse, which you never see them on these babes in the five-and-ten-cent stores. Plus a patrician instep that bespeaks five hundred years of breeding.

CHARISMA (*bursting into tears*): Oh, I'm so tired of adulation! Do you know what it means to have men constantly shooting themselves for love of you, slavering over you, pawing you? I loathe the smell of their cigars in the curtains. Hence I became a writer.

RICKY: But you said you were a designer.

CHARISMA: Labels, badges! What are they but rotten little handcuffs that society fastens on the creative to strangulate their genius? Were I to meet someone with the divine afflatus, be he poet, painter, or dustman, then, by my halidom, I would flee with same to the ends of the earth.

RICKY: Take care lest you fling your cap over the moon. If you met them in a closet like this, they might be an exterminator —a dry cleaner.

CHARISMA: 'Twould matter not a groat, by my maidenhead. Anyhow, getting back to basics, what do you think of my book so far?

RICKY: What book is that?

CHARISMA: Why, *She Spins to Conquer*, which, albeit unfinished, has already reduced Virginia Kirkus to superlatives and netted a tidy four hundred Gs for the paperback rights. You've submitted it to a perusal?

RICKY: (*uncomfortably*): No—only browsed it—the first forty pages—

CHARISMA: But you must have a gut reaction. Even the lowest of the low—my podiatrist, the vegetable man in Gristede's—has a gut reaction.

RICKY: Well, I'll level with you. The characters are well drawn, you have a nice sense of plot, but I miss the infrastructure. Who are we rooting for?

CHARISMA: The girl. The part I want Telly Savalas for.

RICKY: Then who plays Cyprian, the boy?

CHARISMA: Telly can play him, too.

RICKY: You don't foresee a collision of identities?

CHARISMA: Well, I'm not wedded to it, but it's a challenge to the designer in me. I'd like to use heaps and heaps of écru satin for the scene where the two of them capture Bryn Mawr.

RICKY: Charisma, did I ever honeyfogle you? Name me one time when I ever sold you out for a lousy commission. You're my ace client—right?

CHARISMA: We've always enjoyed a good working relationship, yes.

RICKY: Then I'll give you my gut reaction. To me that scene is not believable.

CHARISMA: You feel it strains credulity?

RICKY: I didn't say that—

CHARISMA: You did so! (*Sobbing*) I worked over it for weeks. It was the capstone of the arch, the linchpin of the whole story!

RICKY: No, no, the linchpin was the scene with the St. Bernard puppies climbing on Dr. Volk! Listen to me, honey . . .

CHARISMA (*recoiling*): Take your filthy hands off me. How dare you touch someone with my imperious aquiline features, a lineal descendant of the Orlovs, the Potockis, the Poniatowskis?

RICKY: I was carried away. A drop too much vodka . . .

CHARISMA: Goose that I was, all my governess's warnings went for naught. In my father's vast estates in the Crimea, the overseer's whip would have wiped out such an affront.

RICKY: Excuse, Gräfin. I just heard a knock on the door. Should I answer it?

CHARISMA (*acidly*): I'm quite capable of looking after my own closet, thank you.

(*Revealed in the doorway is a soldierly figure, fainting and half exhausted, clad in a military greatcoat. His astrakhan shako has slipped back to disclose a bloodstained bandage.*)

MAN: Is there a Monsieur Tickitavsky here?

RICKY: I am he.

MAN (*saluting*): Sire, I am Michael Strogoff, courier of the Czar; I bear important dispatches from the imperial court. Forgive my appearance, but I have driven many versts. Ricky Petrovich—

RICKY: Enough with the patronymics. Make with the dispatches.

STROGOFF: Here they are, Altesse.

RICKY (*exultantly, as he reads*): Charisma! Sweetheart! Where are you?

CHARISMA: Right here by your shoebox. Is it good news?

RICKY: You better believe it. The thrust is that, following lengthy investigation, it has come to light that Count Boris Przystalski, the wealthiest landholder in the Crimea, and I were switched in our cradles by a scheming quadroon. As the real Count Boris, I now possess twelve thousand serfs, a goodly sum in cash, and his entire fief.

CHARISMA: Oh, Ricky, how super. We always dreamt of having our own fief.

RICKY: Yes, it's magic. Only in an American closet could such a thing happen, a baseborn Litvak winning a shiksa of royal lineage.

STROGOFF (*impatiently*): Is there any answer for the Czar? I can't stand here cooling my steeds all night. They're flecked with foam.

RICKY: How do you like that? A greenhorn, an apple-knocker, and already he's burning up the freeways. Where's the fire?

STROGOFF: I'm huddling with Francis Ford Coppola, Norman

Lear, and Swifty Lazar in the Polo Lounge to lens a thirty-nine-week spinoff from my sensational X-rated *Nudity in Varsovie.*

CHARISMA: Who's doing the clothes, if any? Ricky and I just conceived a thrilling new line of see-through jumpsuits yclept Schmottas Polonaises.

STROGOFF: Then you got yourself a deal, Countess. Follow me!

(The three link arms and hasten excitedly toward the Polo Lounge.)

CURTAIN

The Joy of Mooching

To Mombasa, Mogadishu, and Modesto I have been; to Montecatini, Montenegro, and Monaco; but never, wide-ranging *Wandervogel* though I pride myself on being, have I set foot in Monza. A town northeast of Milan and slightly northwest of Gorgonzola, on the road to Bergamo, Monza has as its chief industry, as far as I can make out, the export of curiosa to the world press. Here are born those strange and often lunatic fillers that piece out the news stories one reads, such as the paragraph that filtered into the *Times* a while ago: "Monza, Italy (AP) — Ambrogio Bacis, 69 years old, does not like dentists, so to pull an aching tooth he fastened a cord to the tooth and the other end to an automobile bumper, and started the car. Mr. Bracis's head collided with the bumper, and he wound up in the hospital, with the tooth still in his mouth." To my way of thinking, the classical Tom Sawyer extraction—the silk thread tied to the bedstead, the hot coal brandished in the patient's face—remains unsurpassed in home dentistry, but obviously Bacis, in his anxiety to be up to date, opted for a fifteen-hundred-pound Imbroglio. Ah, well, *autres temps, autres mœurs*.

Another and even more seductive item emanating from Monza turned up in *The Jerusalem Post* recently; to wit: "It must rank as one of the strangest cocktail parties ever—and it was thrown by well-dressed Sebastiano Amara, of Monza, Italy, to boost sales of a book he's just published, *How to Make*

47

Begging Pay. The suave author and man-about-town received his guests, doled out liberal Martinis, then begged to be excused. In a few minutes he returned—disguised as a crippled beggar, his face contorted with agony as he hobbled in on crutches. Guests in cars then followed 25-year-old Sebastiano to Monza's main shopping street, watched as he laid his crutches on the pavement and started weeping. In ten minutes he had collected the equivalent of $15. In his book he claims he never collected less than $100 a day, and says, 'I did it as a part-time job, mainly for aesthetic pleasure, and only partly for pocket money.' "

My initial response to Signor Amara's exploit was, I must confess, one of jealousy. Myself a suave author and man-about-town, I was piqued that I hadn't conceived so original a method of publicizing my own books. As envy subsided, though, one phrase of his kept pestering me like a caraway seed embedded in a tooth (a dental metaphor doubtless arising from Mr. Bacis's predicament): that he had acted thus "mainly for aesthetic pleasure." Now, among various paragons on whom I have modelled myself from time to time—the Scarlet Pimpernel, the Earl of Rochester, Baruch Spinoza—one of the more influential was Des Esseintes, the hero of Joris Karl Huysmans' *Against the Grain*, who ceaselessly sought artistic stimulus in drugs, perfumes, and vice. Was it possible that this scribbler on the road to Bergamo had experienced in mendicancy a psychic release overlooked by Des Esseintes and me, deftly fattening his royalties meanwhile? Unimaginable, I told myself, but still I ought to lose no time in emulating him, and I fell to work.

As a neophyte in the world of beggary, I decided that the role best suited to me was traditional. Accordingly, I purchased a ragged shawl and a size-12 gingham dress from a pushcart on Rivington Street, and issued invitations to a half-dozen friends for cocktails at my hotel on Gramercy Park. At the height of the party, while my guests were feverishly consuming Martinis and bandying epigrams, I excused myself, retired to the bedroom, and transformed myself into a waif. The conversion was not wholly successful, as the little match girl in the fairy tale of Hans Christian Andersen is rarely depicted with a mustache, but nonetheless I resolved to brazen it out. To my gratification, the effect on the assemblage was volcanic. Everyone literally stood rooted to the floor.

"*Voyons!* A supreme master of illusion!" I heard people exclaiming. "Another Lon Chaney! Can our eyes be deceiving us? In a few expert strokes, this *arbiter elegantiarum* has, as it were, metamorphosed himself into a vag."

Like Sebastiano, I would have liked my intimates to follow me in their motors, but, as none of them owned any, I bade them go on drinking—a somewhat empty gesture, since the bottles were exhausted—and took my leave. Crossing to the south side of Gramercy Park, I stationed myself with my tray of matches outside The Players Club. The circumstances, I saw at once, were unpropitious. Ideally, it should have been snowing; instead, it was a hot, sultry evening, beckoning the passerby to Baskin-Robbins for an ice-cream cone rather than to contribute alms. After a while, a gentleman came out of the club, placing his feet with great deliberation, in the manner of one who has dined well on glazed Virginia ham with sweet potatoes.

"Please, sir, buy my matches," I whined. "Owing to a conspiracy among the reviewers, my latest book is already on the eighty-nine-cent table at Barnes & Noble. Have pity on me—don't let them recycle it. Also, I write by gaslight, and Consolidated Edison is threatening to cut off the gas. Support the arts, even if, as I suspect, you can barely support yourself."

My prospect gaped at me incredulously and, muttering to himself, went back into the club. An ashen-haired model in three shades of denim, leading an ashen-haired borzoi, approached; as they neared me, the dog sat down growling and she pulled him past with an apologetic "Sorry, he hates beggars" that at least certified that my disguise was valid. Then two character actors, their brows furrowed by unemployment, emerged from The Players. Sucking in my cheeks to simulate the ravages of hunger, I bore down on them.

" 'A benison, playgoers, a cornucopia! A feast for the intelligence!' " I snuffled. "That is what the New York critics wrote about my last play—amateur rights now available from Samuel French, Incorporated. And how many scripts have they sold? Three lousy copies! How am I to sustain myself, to wield my pen in the tradition of Congreve, Sheridan, and Wilde, without your philanthropic assistance? Buy my vestas, I implore you."

"Beat it, chump," the elder of the pair countered roughly. "Save those hard-luck stories for the Bowery. Write yourself a soap for Procter & Gamble, or go on relief, like the rest of us."

Crestfallen and perspiring from the heat of the shawl, I shambled back to the hotel and sat down to rethink a modus operandi. Could it be, I asked myself, that the persona I had chosen was too depressing, that people would be more generous if the nature of my plight were bizarre or offbeat? To the fiery temperament, decision is consonant with action; in a trice I divested myself of my rags, slipped into a dinner jacket, and, faultlessly arrayed in black silk hose but no slippers, shot uptown in a taxi. Dismounting between two expensive Park Avenue apartments in the Sixties, I took up a stand near the canopy of the more opulent. Several cabs arrived bearing couples and parties, but I ignored them. At length, one discharged a jovial, fortyish individual with a worldly air, smoking a Perfecto. I accosted him furtively.

"Excuse me, friend, but I'm in a bit of a jam. Might we have a word?"

His eyes encompassed my garb, widened at my stockinged feet. "What is it?"

"Well," I confided, chuckling in hearty man-to-man fashion, "the fact is, I was having a slap and a tickle with a certain married lady in this building whose identity must be protected at all costs. I mean, we're all human, what? As the fellow said, who's to cast the first stone?"

"Yes, yes," he said impatiently. "So her husband came home

unexpectedly and you left just in the nick without your pumps. Where do I fit into this?"

"Wait. I was coming to that." I swallowed. "You see, I'm a writer by profession, and I'm supposed to autograph my new best-seller at Doubleday's for admirers, but I can't let them see me like this. Unfortunately, though, I forgot my wallet upstairs, too. If you could lend me the price of a new pair—"

He cut me short with a paternal hand on my sleeve. "Shape up, brother," he said. "You're not a writer—you're a schmo. Anyone that leaves their shoes and their wallet in a lady's boudoir is a butterfingers. Take my advice—if you want to play Lothario, go join the Actors Studio." He shook his head commiseratingly and melted into the foyer.

Dashed though I was by his rebuff, I was not minded to give up so easily, and I squared my jaw. Of the next two arrivals, the first rejected my appeal on the ground that no shoe stores were open at that hour; the second derisively demanded the name of my inamorata. In nineteen years' residence in the house, he said, he had yet to see a female worthy of pursuit. As if to make matters worse, it shortly came on to rain, and by the time I reached home in my wet socks I had such a cold that laryngologists skyed in from as far away as Mayo to study it.

During the long, slow convalescence that followed, I stewed over my inability to equal Sebastiano's receipts or to glean even a mite of aesthetic pleasure from the process. At last, I hit on the reason. The identities I had chosen, match girl and philanderer, were too foreign to my nature. Temperamentally a dreamer and a rover, I was trying to be a schnorrer, too, which was altogether alien, for *au fond* I was prouder than a Spanish hidalgo and would accept alms from no man. It was out of character—as if Lord Olivier were to impersonate Pecksniff and then pass the hat. Ergo, I must not dissemble; I must boldly admit myself a genius whose wares were unsalable, a drug on the market, and if that shamed an apathetic public into showering me with gold, I could with dignity accept my rightful due. Immediately a weight lifted from my shoulders. Donning the velvet jacket, Windsor tie, and beret I normally wear when writing, I hurried to the Marboro bookshop on West Eighth Street. Rapture—my suspicion was confirmed; an unsold pile of my most recent opus, reduced to fifty-nine cents, loomed up higher than a ziggurat. Folding my arms, I took up a position alongside it and waited to be pitied.

Half an hour passed and nobody appeared—not even a kleptomaniac. Finally, a heavily bearded man in a filthy Confederate tunic, who looked like Colonel Mosby but proved to be a youth of seventeen, materialized and asked the clerk for a primer on flagellation. A couple of teen-agers with schoolbags came in, leafed through Eberhard and Phyllis Kronhausen's *Pornography and the Law*, and left, sniffing disappointedly. A stout yenta in picador dress but minus leather chaps exchanged a copy of Sara Kasdan's *Love and Knishes* for a poster of Donatello's David. With that, all activity halted, and I grew hot under the collar. My patience was ebbing fast.

"Hey, General Guderian, what gives here?" I queried the uniformed guard sporting a nightstick. "Where are the browsers?"

"Nobody gets up before noon in the Village," he said. "Takes a while for the marijuana fumes to clear."

In due course, the pace altered; shoppers, most of them somnambulists, started drifting through the aisles, languidly fingering the bargains and striving to read the erotica sealed in cellophane. Posed by my works, I assumed an expression at once dismal and haughty, insouciant yet despondent, that would have wrung the stoniest heart. But naught booted me, truth to tell, for as the illiterate swine neared my books their faces hardened and they sheared off, burying their noses in the fescennine pages of Harold Robbins and Irving Wallace. Resolved that those who had died for literature should not have fallen in vain, I determined to speak out.

"So the philistines have triumphed again, have they?" I

began, raising my voice. "What price now Kafka in his garret, Melville eking out his days as a customs inspector? Was it for this that Keats—"

Suddenly the words died in my throat; a Lincolnian figure I recognized as—or took to be—Philip Roth's had entered the door and was scanning the counters for remaindered copies of his books. He did not have to scan long, because adjacent to mine stood another ziggurat, even taller and likewise discounted, of *The Great American Novel*. In the same instant, his quick novelist's eye discerned what I was doing and he strode angrily toward me.

"Scab! Cut-rate fink!" he exploded. "So this is how you dispose of your overstock, by appealing to the sentimental side of your non-readers!"

"For shame, mealymouth!" I flung back. "Who are you to criticize? You were just sneaking in to push your own remainders. I at least was bent on deriving aesthetic pleasure from my humiliation."

"Oho!" he jeered. "Uncontent with being a dreamer and a rover, you're a masochist, too. My psychiatrist has an ugly name for that!"

"You don't say," I returned, interested. "What is it?"

"Well, I forget, actually," he said, "but I'll give you his phone number—you can ask him."

"Gee, that's nice of you, Roth," I said. "Look here, I'd like to inscribe one of my books for you."

"And I for you," he said, doing so and handing it to me. "Listen, if you're going uptown, why don't we split a cab? After all, between us we sold a couple of books this afternoon."

And that, plus a talk we had about girls over a glass of tea at the Belmore Cafeteria, is the sum total of what I gleaned from patterning myself on the author of *How to Make Begging Pay*. Well, I hope his manual sells like hotcakes in Monza and never gets remaindered. Because if the silly beggar comes around to me for sympathy, I'll tell him a thing or two.

Recapture Your Rapture,
in One Seedy Session

Loath though I am to bring *The New York Review of Books*, *The Times Literary Supplement*, and the academics buzzing down around my ears like a cloud of hornets, I'd like to ask a simple question. Why is it that in the torrent of acclamation, exegesis, and criticism which has gushed forth during this century about Proust's monumental *Remembrance of Things Past* we find not so much as a mention of the Steinberg theory? It may come as a surprise to those who regard him as merely a gifted artist to learn that Mr. Saul Steinberg has thought long and deeply about the catalytic agent of the novel. (I do not refer to Gaston Farblondget, the playbroker who first brought it to the attention of Grasset, the original publisher, but, rather, to the pastry, the *madeleine* soaked in lime-flower tea, that evoked the author's recollections.) Nevertheless, Mr. Steinberg has, and it is his contention, iconoclastic if you will, that Proust deliberately falsified what he had eaten as being too plebeian. In Steinberg's judgment—and he buttresses it with a formidable array of interior evidence from the work—Proust's *madeleine* was in reality a matzo ball, and the past unfolded itself to the Master as he sat hunched over a bowl of chicken soup in Flambaum's, the famous kosher restaurant in Paris.

Absurd, you say? Improbable? Yet scientific researchers, people like L. Ron Hubbard, Jeane Dixon, and William Safire, who have spent years studying the intricacies of the human brain, tell us that one's own skein of memory often starts unwinding under similarly mundane circumstances. Such was undeniably the case with me several months ago in the basement workshop of a bootmaker in London's West End, twenty feet below the surface of Cork Street. I had crawled down there on a rainy afternoon to pick up some shoelaces he had rehabilitated for me, and, as was his habit of late, Mr. Bloodroot launched into a gloomy discourse on the decline of his calling. In the best of times, Bloodroot has never displayed a tincture of optimism, and today his wrinkled visage was more doleful than a basset hound's. Vanished forever, he declaimed, were apprentices willing to school themselves in the discipline of shoecraft, vanished the client with discernment and the means to appreciate superb workmanship. Was this subterranean badger hole we stood in an adequate reward for his years of unremitting industry? Apprehensive lest the man disembowel himself with an awl before my eyes, I appealed to his *amour-propre*.

"But think of the clientele you've had, sir," I protested. "Sir Winston, Duff Cooper, the Sitwells—"

"Oh, aye, I've made for them all," he agreed sombrely. "And the actors, too. Olivier, Gielgud, and Redgrave—the lot."

"Yes, and what about the American film stars? I daresay you've known plenty of them, like Clark Gable and Douglas Fairbanks, Jr."

From his instant disdain, I saw that his pride had been touched. "Fairbanks? He was a nobody compared to some of my customers. Look here." He fumbled out a battered cardcase, shuffled the contents, and handed me a creased and yellowed letter. "You've heard of *him*, I expect."

I had indeed. Dated March 14, 1921, the note was addressed from North Roxbury Drive, in Beverly Hills. "Dear Mr. Bloodroot," it read. "I trust that this finds you well. I would like at this time to order another pair of the patent-leather shoes with gray cloth tops, buttoning on the side, which you supplied me in the past. Will forward international money order on receipt. With kindest regards, Rudolph Valentino."

Valentino the incomparable—the immortal Rudy, with his glittering snake eyes and hair ebony as the raven's wing, his feline grace; the image of those shoes brought him surging across the gulf of years as nothing else could. Dazzled, I toiled back to sidewalk level from Bloodroot's den and, over a pint of Guinness to offset the bends, gave myself up to memories of the Sheik of Araby. Certainly the most vivid, if not the first, was that of his performance as a torero in *Blood and Sand* about 1922, when he twirled across his dressing room like a teetotum to gird himself in a silver sash held by an attendant. His leading lady, of course, was the divine Nita Naldi, and, by a nice coincidence, light had been shed only recently on the reason for her choice. Reporting on a Dublin film festival, David Robinson, the movie critic of *The Times* of London, told this story:

The exotic Latin vamp of the 1920s, Nita Naldi was, it appears, really called Anita Dooley. She first encountered the literary lion of the day, Blasco Ibanez, at a party, and as a good Irish Catholic girl upbraided him roundly for his treatment of the Church. The argument became so heated that the great man's false teeth flew out and straight down Miss Naldi's corsage [which, Mr. Robinson unaccountably neglected to add, was unrivalled in the Western world save by Aileen Pringle's]. Without pausing for breath, Ibanez plunged his hand into the crevasse, retrieved his teeth and clapped them back into his mouth. Evidently the experience had made an impression on him, however, for he insisted that Miss Naldi should star opposite Rudolph Valentino in the film of his novel "Blood and Sand."

Nita Naldi, Wallace Reid, Olga Petrova, Owen Moore, Priscilla Dean, Beverly Bayne, Dustin Farnum, Rosemary Theby, Valeska Suratt—a kaleidoscope of faces swarm up from my early moviegoing to tighten my throat. And, bathed in a flood of sweet melancholy underscored by the throb of violins, I was struck by an awesome thought: I was probably the only surviving member of the Rhode Island audience that witnessed the original screen version of *Anna Karenina* in 1916. This cinematic douche, my baptism in the medium, took place in a malodorous nickelodeon in Providence, the seats of which bore cassettes that ejected Tootsie Rolls with an explosive force like gunfire. The production starred a Danish actress of surpassing loveliness named Betty Nansen—unrelated to the Arctic explorer, except that her beauty froze me in my chair. That Anna's romance with Count Vronsky was star-crossed was apparent to me even at the age of twelve, but when she threw herself under the wheels of the locomotive in the last reel, I fell apart. Blubbering piteously, I stumbled homeward in a mist of tears, and lay between life and death for weeks. Eventually, thanks to nourishing soups and the delicious humor of Octavus Roy Cohen in *The Saturday Evening Post*, I regained my zest for life, but it was a narrow squeak.

Figure to yourself, then, how spooky I felt when, several days after my visit to Bloodroot, there fell into my hands at a curio shop in St. Martin's Lane a magazine for British movie exhibitors published in 1913. By and large, the trade gossip in *The Cinema News & Property Gazette*, the advertisements for pipe organs, ticket machines, and similar embellishments were nothing to quicken the pulse, but the suggestion column did offer one method of attracting summer patrons which was worthy of note:

The man with the screen at one end of a vacant lot and a projection room at the other [will be] in the ascendant. . . . A rockery need not cost £2, and yet it will be worth a hundred times that in the suggestion of coolness that it affords. Tap the water pipe, and put in a small hose nozzle. Build a concrete basin. Even a galvanized washtub with an overflow pipe will do. Some Saturday afternoon get in half a dozen small boys, and promise them tickets for the entire opening week if they will gather up the stones in the lot. They'll work like grownups if you pick the right sort of boys, and by night you'll have a fine pile of stones. Mask in the basin and pipe with these, adjust the nozzle so that some of the spray strikes the rocks, and you'll have a tiny fountain that will splash musically.

How to dispose of the pile of small boys left over after the opening week was unclear, but I assume the stiffs could be paid off in stones and the brighter ones used as ushers. Where the publication really took wing, though, was in its listing of films marketed by various European and American studios, synopsized in language even the most beef-witted exhibitor could comprehend. Included were some with juicy titles, like *The Blind Composer's Dilemma* (Kalem), *While She Powdered Her Nose* (Vitagraph), *The Newest Methods of Coaling Battleships at Sea* (Edison), *Tony's Revenge, or Castor Oil* (Elite), *Cub Reporter's Temptation* (Kalem), *Oh! You Unbreakable Doll* (Lux), and *Saved from the Grip of Alcohol* (Lux). Of the plots furnished in this issue, comedies were preponderant; there were few problem dramas, the producers obviously leaning toward boisterous situations spiced with a dash of sex. Here, typically, was a Selig Polyscope film called *The College Chaperon*, whose ingenious twists were guaranteed to elicit boffs:

The annual college dance is at hand, and the students of the Conserver Military Academy are making their arrangements for this famous function. Jack Carter and Ned Graves invite two out-of-town girls to be their guests at the festivities. The girls, Maude and Alice, accept the boys' invitation, with the understanding that Jack's Aunt Nellie will act as their chaperon. It is so arranged, and preparations made accordingly. Shortly before the eventful day, Jack is notified that Aunt Nellie cannot be present. The boys are much put out at this bit of news, and are about to call the engagement off, when suddenly a bright idea occurs to them. They arrange with Sammy Stone, the college janitor, to impersonate Aunt Nellie. Sammy consents, and plays the part. Outside of several embarrassing situations that arise, the scheme works out all right until Sammy, in his elaborate ball gown, attempts to dance with one of the professors. His identity is discovered, and he lands in the guard house. Here the boys visit him, and offer their condolences to "one of our best little chaperons."

Judging from the background of two other pictures. *The Story of Lavinia* (Selig) and *Luggage in Advance* (Barker), dormitories, and, above all, female ones, pullulated with comedy; both these divertissements featured clandestine chafing-dish parties, pillow fights, male intruders concealed in laundry baskets, and similar low jinks. *The Thief and the Porter's Head*

(Milano), however, classified as a blithesome comic melodrama, proved in the end to be a quite different bouillabaisse:

Mr. and Mrs. Jones are suddenly called away, and leave their son, Percy, alone in the house. Left alone, he helps himself to his father's cigars, and reckons he is quite a nut, until, overcome by the strength of the smoke, he lies down on the sofa. Meanwhile a thief, seeing the departure of Mr. and Mrs. Jones, breaks into the house and frightens Percy, who beats a hasty retreat, being chased from room to room by the thief, until at last he is cornered. . . . Percy slings a pot of paint after him which alights on his head. The thief pulls it off and bangs it down over the head of the porter, who has rushed out to find the cause of the row, and decamps. Mr. and Mrs. Jones return at this point, and Percy rushes down and says he has caught a thief; they catch hold of the pot to pull it off, and succeed in also pulling off the head of the porter. The unfortunate man rushes round with his head, still encased in the pot in his hand, to the doctor, and the rest of the party follow. The doctor succeeds, by the aid of electricity, in sticking his head on again, and upon the pot being smashed, they discover not the thief as they expected, but the porter, and at once proceed to inflict their wrath on Percy. The doctor, getting sick of the rowdy crowd, throws his electric plug into the mob and disperses them.

Surrealism, I had always naïvely supposed, was fathered during the twenties by Max Ernst, René Magritte, Pierre Roy, and like effervescent spirits, but revelations of headless porters in 1913 and doctors welding heads back on with electricity are certain to ruffle the weathers of art historians. I wonder if moviegoers in that distant epoch, torpidly gnawing their Tootsie Rolls, dreamt they were watching the birth of a new art form. Or did they accept weird fantasies flickering across the screen as part of its incomprehensible magic? However glazed, their eyes must have bulged at an Essanay feature titled *Lady Audley's Jewels,* a succulent ragout of show biz and crime detection:

Augustus Pompleton and his wife, Clarice Deveraux of the famous McNight's Celebrated Repertoire Company, are stranded in the small village of Jayville. Pompleton, at the suggestion of his wife, enters the railroad station and asks the ticket agent where they can find the nearest and cheapest hotel. The star leading lady of the noted company drops her lavaliere, made of plate glass and paste, on the floor. The station agent picks it up and asks her how much she will sell it for. The lavaliere is sold for three dollars. Jed Perkins, a would-be sleuth of the town, receives a badge, belt, handcuffs and the regular paraphernalia used by town constables from a detective correspondence school. A five hundred thousand dollar jewel robbery adorns the front page of a New York newspaper. Having secured enough money to hold them over at the hotel for a couple of days, Augustus Pompleton and his wife register and go to their room, to determine how to reach New York. During the absence of the porter, Perkins volunteers to take some ice water up to them. He discovers the performers sorting out some stage jewels. He immediately comes to the conclusion that these two are the thieves wanted in New York in connection with the big robbery. The actors carry out the misunderstanding, and are taken to New York by the correspondence sleuth. Having arrived at the police station, the Captain discharges the couple and has the would-be detective locked up.

The one perplexing aspect of the story—apart from the puzzle of where the producer promoted the funds to make it—is the identity of Lady Audley, who never once surfaces in the summary of the action. Presumably, she is the owner of the gems heisted in New York, a detail whose concealment somebody evidently figured would add a touch of mystery to the script. The practice of withholding information from the audience still persists, by the way; I frequently emerge from movies convinced that some vital ingredient that would explain the whole tzimmes has been deliberately suppressed.

The more one samples the fare offered the cinemagoer in 1913, the greater one's admiration for his ability to endure punishment. Dazzled as he undoubtedly was by the witchery of the new medium, he must have staggered under the impact of some of the lunacies it generated, such as those in *In a Gambler's Clutches* (Atlas Feature Films). Its story line, for want of a better phrase, went as follows:

Rigo Seriesky, a famous violinist, fascinates Marie, the daughter of Baron Schulbert. He asks for Marie's hand in marriage, but the Baron, who has been warned that Seriesky is a common adventurer and card-sharper, refuses his consent. Rigo sends a message to Marie by means of her dog, asking her to elope with him.

This novel deputy, by the way, may be the very first appearance of that folkloric figure, the talking dog, which inspired a host of anecdotes to come. But go on with the narrative:

She agrees, and at midnight they run away and are secretly married. A year later Rigo forces Marie to accompany him to a gambling saloon. He makes her cheat by using cards concealed in her handkerchief, and the fraud being discovered, Rigo is challenged to a duel by one of the gamblers. During the duel Rigo is wounded in the arm, and when the wound is healed he finds to his horror that his arm is paralyzed and useless.

You spring to attention, foreseeing that they are about to use the classic dreidel wherein the hands of an executed strangler are grafted onto a concert pianist—but no, this was long before the era of Tod Browning and Robert Siodmak. Slowly, relentlessly, the story unwinds like some anaconda in the Amazon rain forest:

Ruin stares him in the face, and Rigo, in desperation, forms a dastardly scheme. At the revolver's mouth he forces his wife to telephone to her father, telling him that she is ill, and imploring him to visit her. Without hesitation the Baron drives to Rigo's house, where the adventurer shows him into a room, saying he will bring Marie to him. Whilst the Baron is waiting Rigo creeps up behind him and binds him to the chair. Then he prepares to set fire to the house, telling his prisoner that in a few hours the place will be in flames. Taking the Baron's keys, the villain leaves the house, returning in the waiting motor, disguised as the Baron. It is his intention to rob the Baron's safe. Unknown to him, however, Schulbert has protected his property by a new electrical contrivance. Unconscious of the danger he runs, Rigo approaches the safe and places the key in the lock. There is a sudden flash, and the schemer falls to the floor electrocuted.

What with the Wagnerian pianology that accompanied these didos and the percussion of the candy machines, I now readily understand the recurrence of nightmares in my youth. Sleeping, I relived all the fantasies at the matinée and I was in constant flight, obsessed by undefinable guilt. Today, so many decades afterward, *The Cinema News & Property Gazette* provides the key, and I know how the guilt originated—from close identification with chimeras like *Sammy and the Chicken Run* (Urbanora):

An extremely clever picture, in which Sammy scores a great triumph. He, in company with two pals, starts out to steal their dinner. They enter a poultry yard, and catching half a dozen fowls, make off with all speed. The owner, disturbed by the cackling of the chickens, soon discovers the theft, and informing the mayor of his loss, persuades that pompous gentleman to join in the chase. But Sammy and his accomplices are too smart for their pursuers, and get away every time, after allowing themselves to be nearly caught, and in the end turn the tables neatly on the injured citizens.

And yet, you know something? I've just been struck by another awesome thought. That isn't such a bad plot after all; you could update it a little, switch the locale, stick a name or two in the leads, and make yourself a bundle. Just to spitball for a second, say that Robert Redford and Paul Newman are a pair of merchant seamen stranded in the Middle East, at Abu Dhabi or Dubai. They steal a couple of chicks out of the emir's harem and take off on his yacht for Israel. A hue and cry in the U.N., the Third World's on fire, and Kissinger (Rod Steiger) takes off after them to avert a confrontation. Do you buy that so far? Right! . . . Operator! In Beverly Hills, please, the phone number for a catalytic agent on South Beverly Drive by the name of Irving Lazar. Yes, thank you, I'll wait.

Under the Shrinking Royalty the Village Smithy Stands

The oval anteroom of Diamond & Oyster, my publishers, had been refurbished since my last visit with a large bas-relief plaque of their logo, a diamond-studded oyster bearing the motto *"Noli unquam oblivisci, Carole: pecuniam sapientiam esse"* ("Never Forget, Charlie: Money Is Wisdom"), and under it a blond, oval-shaped receptionist strikingly reminiscent of Shelley Winters. As thirty-five minutes ticked away without any word from Mitchell Krakauer, the editor I was calling on, I began to develop paranoid symptoms. Heretofore there hadn't been any hassle about seeing him; what was amiss now? Had some stripling in patched denim fresh out of Antioch whispered into his ear that I was *vieux jeu*, old hat, *nye kulturny*? Or had Krakauer learned in some devious way that Shelley Winters was in a 1941 play of mine, *The Night Before Christmas*, and deliberately planted her double here to taunt me as a slippered pantaloon? I felt myself inflate like a blowfish at the veiled insult. Surely nobody could be so base, and yet in this carnivorous age of four-hundred-thousand-dollar sales and instant remainders worship of the bitch goddess Success overrode a decent respect for the aged. I got to my feet, cheeks flaming.

"Try Mr. Krakauer's line again, Miss. I can't understand why they don't answer."

The receptionist's eyes rolled upward in martyrdom. "Look,

sir, do I have to keep on telling you? If you'd only state your business—"

"My dear young woman," I said, gripping the edge of her desk to steady myself. "Since you were in amniotic fluid when I first signed with this house, let me enlighten you. Diamond & Oyster have published eleven books of mine. If I have to undergo a Rorschach to discuss a twelfth, maybe it's time I peddled my papers elsewhere."

"Oh, you're one of our *authors!*" she squealed. "Why didn't you mention that before? Who did you say you were?"

"Well, my real name is Travis Nuthatch, but I write under the name of Israel Zangwill."

"O.K., Mr. Zangwill. You have a seat there, and I'll see what I can do."

She busied herself with her apparatus, and I sat down, mollified and refreshed by our interchange. More time passed. Messengers innumerable arrived laden with proofs, drawings, and office lunches. Three or four lovelies from Vassar and Bennington, job applicants hugging postgraduate degrees in Middle English and Georgian poetry to their enchanting bosoms, passed through to be interviewed and dated by lickerish subordinates. A whole decrepitude of writers—Sudanese, Lapps, Bosnians, Trobrianders—appeared and were hustled in on their own recognizance, and still I sat there, a pariah excluded from the temple of letters he had helped erect. Then a sobering thought struck me. In all justice to Krakauer, he had no appointment with me; I'd come by on an impulse, without phoning, and perhaps he was in a meeting, or, more likely, on the bridle path. Krakauer's passion for horsemanship was a byword—he was besotted with the sport. His office was filled with stirrups, snaffles, and trophies attesting to his equestrian skill; he wore riding breeches to work, swished a crop against them as he conferred. Still, wherever he was at the moment, I thought sullenly, it ill behooved his secretary to keep a celebrity like Israel Zangwill, dead *or* alive, cooling his heels in the anteroom.

"Hello there!" a familiar British voice exclaimed. "What in the world are you doing here?" The owner of the voice was a florid, dapper gentleman with a Guard's mustache, clad in a short warm. "Remember me? Arthur Maybrick, of Edouard & Russell, your haberdashers in Clifford Street?"

"To be sure," I said, rising. "How are you? I heard you retired when the firm closed down."

"Couldn't stand the inactivity. I'm with Tautz nowadays—you recall, the sporting tailors who used to be in Grafton Street. Matter of fact, that's why I'm here. Just had a word with Mitchell Krakauer. Do you know him?"

Curious to ascertain what publishers buy one half so precious as the thing they sell, I clamored for details. In a recent sale at Parke Bernet, it emerged, Krakauer, after fierce bidding, had acquired a pair of breeches made by Tautz for John Huston when he was M.F.H. of the Galway Blazers in Ireland. As Krakauer was two feet shorter than Huston, substantial alterations were necessary crotchwise, and Maybrick had been flown overseas to superintend them. "What with my fare and hotel expenses, it'll come to a neat eight hundred quid before we're done," he told me, "but I must say I haven't heard a peep out of the man."

"Neither have I. I've been waiting here over an hour."

"I say," remarked Maybrick, voice lowered. "Rather weird setup he has in there for a publisher's office, don't you think?"

"How do you mean—the horse brasses and so forth?"

"No, no, the other stuff," he said mysteriously. "Ah, well, I daresay you'll see for yourself."

"Ready for you, Mr. Zangwill," the receptionist fluted. "You can go in now."

With a handshake and an injunction to knock him up on my next visit to London, Maybrick left and I went down the hall. Calpurnia, Krakauer's secretary, rose from her typewriter as I entered. She was wearing not only a bowler and a stock but a riding apron that seemed excessive for the amount of mud kicked up on the twenty-eighth floor of a skyscraper.

"Oh, it's you," she said, and added, puzzled, "Where's Mr. Zangwill?"

I shrugged. *¿Quién sabe?* That's one of those metaphysical

questions." I nodded toward the interior. "Is Mitchell free now?"

"He will be in a jiffy. He's just finishing something."

I subsided, and, reaching for a copy of *The Field*, buried myself in its pages. Halfway through an article on the paucity of oasthouses in East Anglia, I stiffened. A deep repeated wheezing, like giant inhalations of breath, was proceeding from Krakauer's sanctum, followed by the clang of metal being struck. Alarmed, I turned toward Calpurnia, but she was typing away, visibly undisturbed. Moments later, her phone buzzed and she motioned me inward.

So startling was the transformation I beheld that my mouth fell open. The burled-walnut desk, the luxurious easy chairs and sporting prints, the equestrian memorabilia—all had vanished, and in their place was a scene straight out of Longfellow: a miniature nineteenth-century blacksmith shop. Garbed in a leather apron, Krakauer was bent over an anvil, his hammer busily tapping a horseshoe. Spread all about were the traditional accoutrements of the smith—the forge heaped with glowing coals, the bellows, pincers, a workbench strewn with tools, and bundles of iron bars.

"Come in, man, come in!" Krakauer hailed me cheerily, laying aside his hammer. He wiped the honest sweat from his brow with a bandanna, extracted a square of cut plug. "Have a chaw?"

I shook my head, still overcome. "Jiminy, what's happened? Nobody told me—I mean, where am I?"

"I know," he said. "Everyone was stunned when I made the change, but I guess you've been away, eh? Well, sit down somewhere—do you mind this soapbox?—and I'll put you in the picture."

"Before you do, though," I asked, "what business are you in?"

"Oh, I still publish, but in a different way. I take it you know who Gaston Gallimard was?"

"Sure, the famous French publisher. Didn't he die last year?"

"Right. He brought out Proust, Gide, Sartre, Malraux—you name it. Well, just prior to his death, at ninety-four, here's what

. he said." He handed me a newspaper clipping encased in plastic. "This was his obit in the London *Times*. Read the last paragraph."

" 'If I could have my life over again,' " it ran, " 'I would choose as a first occupation something having nothing to do with publishing, say a pharmacist's or plumber's business. There the income would allow me to publish on the side only all that pleased me without having to think in the slightest about the commercial side.' "

"And you've actually realized his dream," I marvelled.

"I've tried. Of course, pharmacy and plumbing take years of study, but spending half my life in the saddle as I do, all this"— he gestured about—"is practically second nature to me. And you'd be surprised the income I make from horseshoes. Not to be sneezed at."

"But how many good noncommercial books have you discovered?"

"None so far," he admitted, folding his arms. "But just look at my biceps. You won't find brawny arms like these over at Knopf or Viking. Anyway, enough about me. Do I sense you have a new book in the oven?"

"Mitchell," I said. "I don't want to crow, but this is going to be the biggest thing since *Les Misérables*—it'll yield three printings before publication. The central character is another Jean Valjean. I can see Jack Nicholson in the part—"

"For Chrissake, I told you I'm through with best-sellers. I want something doomed, with an aura of failure."

"It's got that, too," I said urgently. "It's got lust, brutality, compassion, foreign intrigue, suspense—the entire gamut of human emotion. The notion came to me in London last summer."

He retrieved his hammer. "Mind if I go on working while you tell it?"

"No, just so long as you stay in the room. O.K., here's how I latched on to the idea. Back in July, I'm stopping at Brown's Hotel, in Mayfair, and in their house organ, a sheet called

Chandelier, I read that Colonel Sanders, the founder of Kentucky Fried Chicken, has also based himself there. During his last stay, he opened the hundredth Kentucky Fried Chicken store in the U.K., held major press conferences, visited Windsor Castle, lunched at the House of Lords, and picnicked at Woburn Abbey. This cat is a real celebrity in Britain, like—well, like Israel Zangwill."

Krakauer blinked. "Odd you should mention him. I just got word he was coming in to see me."

"Fantastic. But what happened then was even stranger. As I step into the hotel lift an hour later, who's riding down but Colonel Sanders himself—white goatee, string tie, the whole shtick—and another guy, a business associate like. And this bird is strenuously urging the Colonel to buy a bunch of shares in Frank Perdue's chicken empire—and force him out of the field. But it's no dice. The old boy keeps shaking his head, and finally comes out with a slang phrase—a British expression they never heard south of the Mason-Dixon line. 'No, suh,' he says. 'That's all my eye and Betty Martin.' Do you see it, Mitchell? Do you get it?"

"Get what?" He stopped hammering. "He meant it was a lot of blue sky, of bushwa."

"Holy Moses, do I have to spell it out for you? The old guy was a *Limey*—a fake! In a flash, it all dawned on me. Ten to one the real Colonel Sanders was trussed up like a fowl upstairs while these two highbinders were scurrying off to manipulate his stock in a power play netting millions! *Voom*—right away, before we hit the ground floor, I've got my whole novel blocked out. The main story line, the two Colonel Sanderses, is a piece of cake; I can life the plot of E. Phillips Oppenheim's *The Great Impersonation*, weaving in actual real-life characters, like Robert Vesco and Meyer Lansky, the way Doctorow and Capote do. Narrating the action is yours truly, a brilliant young crusading journalist—a combination of Inspector Javert and Leslie Howard—who brings the malefactors to book and wins the Colonel's pulchritudinous niece, Cicely Mainwaring."

"Is any of this on paper yet?"

"Are you out of your living mind?" I snorted. "I should leave a gilt-edged yarn lying around where some goniff from the Authors League can filch it?"

"Yes, that's wise. But there's a better reason not to write it down. It's too commercial, kid, too *much* of a cinch. Yes, it'll make a bloody fortune, but if that's what you want, you're barking up the wrong tree. A new wind is blowing through Diamond & Oyster, my friend."

"That's not what it says on your logo."

"That thing? I'll let you in on a secret. Max Oyster's nephew is a sign painter—he made it for a seafood restaurant in Queens, but they went bust." He wiped his hands on a bit of cotton waste and draped a paternal arm over my shoulder. "Now, pay close attention. Your next book should deal with your profound mystical revelation in India."

"Did I have one?"

"You must have, in some cockamamie ashram or other you saw—everybody does. Unburden yourself. Write a series of poetic epiphanies about death and copulation with wide margins like Kahlil Gibran—something I can sink my teeth into. I could get stuck with ten thousand copies of a work like that if it were done right."

"But you can't guarantee a book will bomb. Barbara Walters is apt to read a passage by mistake and overnight a million listeners will be yelling for a copy."

"Hmm, you're right. We can't afford to run a risk like that. Look, maybe it shouldn't be on the adult level at all. What about a tender love story between a little girl and a pony, told from the pony's point of view? You know, like *Watership Down* or *Salar the Salmon*?"

"Wait, Mitchell, wait!" I cried out, inspired. "I had a notion a while back—how did it go? I had a title and everything. Now I remember! *Smokey and the Millionaire: The Saga of a Whitefish.*"

"Smokey the whitefish." He rolled it over on his tongue. "I

like it. It smells right, you know what I mean? I can see a whole warehouseful of copies ready to be pulped. Where does it take place?"

"At Barney Greengrass the Sturgeon King, on Amsterdam Avenue. It begins the night before Christmas, and all through the house not a herring is stirring, not even a bloater or a side of Novy. The store is empty of stock except for one lone white-fish, Smokey, shivering in this cold showcase. He's plunged into misery—everyone's home decking the halls with challah, trimming the tree with kosher macaroons, and what does the Yuletide hold for poor Smokey? Refrigeration in a dark store, with a hungry cat leering at him."

"Masterly!" exulted Krakauer. "You know who we'll get to do the jacket? Salvador Dali! Each little bone in Smokey cunningly delineated—"

"What is this—a production meeting?" I interrupted. "I'm trying to tell you a *story*. Well, so, carried along by Smokey's stream of consciousness, we retrace his past—his birth in Lake Superior, spawning with girlfriends, a narrow escape from being devoured by a pike, bilge like that. Then, all of a sudden, a long-forgotten incident comes back to him. A wealthy Grosse Pointe sportsman, while angling there, accidentally hooked into a barrel of cement and was in danger of being pulled overboard."

"What was a barrel of cement doing in the lake?"

"Search me," I said impatiently. "Somebody was standing in it—some hoodlum from the Dion O'Banion mob. Anyway, Smokey realized the sportsman's peril, swam to his rescue, and snapped the line with his teeth. Naturally, the sportsman caught only a glimpse of him, but, eternally grateful, vowed that if it was ever in his power he'd repay his debt to the little fellow.

"Now, then," I continued fluently. "We dissolve to the forty-second floor of the Waldorf Towers, where tuxedo-clad Daniel Mariana Trench, powerful Midwest utilities tycoon and world-famed sportsman, sits alone and desolate on Christmas Eve. All his millions, his forty Rembrandts, the superb specimens of fringe-ear oryx, greater kudu, and Mrs. Gray's lechwe that have fallen to his gun frowning down from the walls are as ashes in his mouth, for he is friendless. The four women he's espoused, the children they've borne him care merely for his money; nowhere is there a soul to whom he can turn for companionship. Finally, with a heavy heart, he summons his motor; *faute de mieux*, he will celebrate the Nativity with a midnight snack. As the superbly appointed Daimler glides through Central Park toward Barney Greengrass's—"

"Stop!" commanded Krakauer. "I'm way ahead of you. I can already hear Trench's hoarse cry of recognition: 'Smokey! Is it really you?' I also know where you stole the plot, but in Shaw's version Androcles never ate the lion."

"Neither does Trench eat Smokey," I said firmly. "We squeeze on the two at the Waldorf Towers before a blazing hearth— maybe with Smokey in a little brown tuxedo—clinking glasses in a toast as the bells usher in the Yule."

For a full five seconds, Krakauer stood immersed in thought. "Nope," he said at last. "It's another Pollyanna story and it'll sell like hotcakes, but I regret we're forced to turn it down— it's too joyous, too upbeat. You created a marvellous mood of despair with Smokey brooding in the showcase—almost like Louis-Ferdinand Céline. I was hoping the cat would get his tongue as well as the rest of him. But you blew it with the bubba-meiseh about Daniel Mariana Trench. It's not for Diamond & Oyster, kid. I'm sorry."

I left him standing by his anvil, an idealist from whose deeply furrowed face the last remnants of a dream had drained away. Then, turning up the collar of my trenchcoat, I trudged out into the rain and went across town to Harcourt Brace Jovanovich.

To Yearn Is Subhuman,
to Forestall Divine

"**B**ut you have to eat *somewhere*, man." Roland Portfolio's voice over the phone, wheedling until now, simmered with impatience. "All I'm asking is meet the boy, have a sandwich with him, listen to his ideas. Is that such a hardship?"

"Roland," I said, struggling for self-control, "will you for God's sake get off my back? I've just finished telling you—this Friday night I'm due in Istanbul to catch a Turkish boat bound for Iskenderun and I'm not even packed yet. I've got a million things to do—convert my air ticket, close up the flat, buy a hot-weather fez—"

"Yes, yes, you sound frantic—"

"I'm not *frantic*," I said, and pounded the desk to prove it. "But the last thing I need right now is a kaffeeklatsch with some dropout from that cinema course at N.Y.U."

"Strobe Fischbyne is not a dropout," he snapped. "He graduated Antioch in three years and he won the top award at the Beaver College Festival for his two abstract films, *Blossomings* and *Mosaic in Bubbles*."

"And he's also your nephew, I reminded him. "O.K., here's what you do. Tell him to send me a nine- or ten-page letter written in longhand, on both sides of the paper, outlining the film he visualizes."

"Why in longhand?" he asked suspiciously. "He can type."

"Because it's harder to read that way," I said. "But it'll help me gauge his personality while I'm scrambling around the ruins of Ephesus. He needn't seal the envelope, because the Turks'll open it anyway looking for coins. Well, Roland, thanks for ringing up—"

"So that's all friendship means to you." Now I was in for it— a jeremiad on my inhumanity, selfishness, and basic trivality. "Look, think back to your own career. When you were a nobody, a punk kid just starting out, didn't anyone ever lend you a helping hand? Didn't anyone, out of the goodness of his heart—"

"Stop!" I said wildly. "All right—O.K.! I can stand anything but that rabbinical intonation of yours. Where is this golden boy?"

W hich, in essence, was how I came to be in the Village one day at nightfall, combing the purlieus of Bleecker Street for a coffeehouse named the The Loony Bin. At long last, I found it, a dank, tenebrous tunnel wedged between an Italian social club and a leather shop catering to bondage freaks. Roland's nephew, predictably, was forty-five minutes late, and by the time he appeared I was so numbed by the sickly-sweet odor of hash and the hard rock blasting out of the jukebox that my choler had wilted. Strobe Fischbyne's dark, hollowed eyes, the wisps of beard depending like Spanish moss from his greenish-white face, and his expression of patient suffering instantly verified what I had foreseen. I was straddled with a Raskolnikov.

"Did you have trouble locating this place?" he asked. "The Village is sort of confusing for strangers."

"Isn't it?" I agreed. "It sure baffled me in 1925, but after thirty years or so on Washington Square I managed to get the hang of it."

He was clearly startled. "You mean you lived here that long ago? What was it like?"

"Oh, mainly fields, a few buildings. Not much virgin forest, though."

"Did you know Eugene O'Neill when he was hanging around those waterfront saloons, and E. E. Cummings?"

"Well, he may have hung around E. E. Cummings, but I think on the whole he preferred women. I believe he married a couple of them."

"I don't understand something," Fischbyne observed, perplexed. "My uncle said you spent most of your time in California. That you worked in Hollywood during the Golden Age."

"Which Golden Age was that?"

"Why, the *thirties*," he said, enunciating as if to a deficient child or someone hard of hearing.

Chagrined that I hadn't brought along an ear trumpet like Foxy Grandpa's, I bade him particularize.

"You know, the era when Thalberg and Scott Fitzgerald, Josef von Sternberg, and all those greats were turning out their classics."

"What about it?"

"Well, there was a tremendous burst of creativity in those years—or weren't you aware of it? The same thing that was going on here at the Round Table in the Algonquin."

The temptation was strong to take the lad on my knee, dry him behind the ears, and correct a few misconceptions, but at my back I seemed to hear a Turkish steamer hurrying near, and I desisted. "Just what did you want to see me about, Fischbyne? Your uncle said you had a brainstorm about a film."

He frowned. "Yes, I've got the overall concept, but the skeletal framework is still nebulous in my mind, so to speak. I thought you might help me come to grips with it." Rummaging in his Zouave regimental jacket, he produced a crumpled bit of newsprint. "This piece in last week's *Variety* kindled my thinking. I'd like your reaction."

Tobe Hooper, young Texan who directed the cult favorite 1974 horror film, "The Texas Chain Saw Massacre" [the item reported], is now at work on his first Hollywood film, "Death Trap," about a

Texas psychopath who feeds people to his pet crocodile. Neville Brand plays the lead role in Mardi Rustam's indie production. . . . Hooper, who seems amused while directing the blood-and-gore antics of Brand stabbing girls with a pitchfork and dumping them into his crocodile pond, compares the film to a horror comic book but also feels that it resembles "Chain Saw" in being "a commercial film that I feel good about. It's much more complex than it seems," says the 33-year-old director. "I tried to establish some kind of motif that carries throughout the show—sometimes that's more important than what you're actually showing."

"Man, that's cool," I said, clutching at the only bit of jargon that seemed applicable. "I wonder if the flick'll still be around when I get back from the Aegean."

"Why, how long are you staying there?"

"Well, I planned on only two months, but I may take up Turkish citizenship now. However, that's beside the point. What's your problem, son?"

His fingers toyed with the tendrils fringing his mouth. "Would you say Hooper's theme is valid?"

"You mean of a psychopath feeding girls to crocodiles?" I shrugged. "O.K. for the raincoat brigade, but rather bland for the longhairs. Still, I daresay he'll beef it up—lay in a couple of shrinks and so forth."

"No, I meant his statement that the motif is more important than what appears on the screen. You agree with that?"

"Emphatically. In my experience, the public is sick and tired of watching actors hugging and kissing. What they're hungry for is motifs."

"Right!" he said warmly. "I was thinking along those lines, too, but I couldn't formulate it until Hooper put it into words. It's a totally new concept in modern cinema."

"Oh, I wouldn't go quite that far. I remember once, during the Golden Age, overhearing three ace directors discuss this very point—William (Wild Bill) Wellman, Billy (Wild Billy) Wilder, and William (Wild Willie) Wyler."

Strobe Fischbyne's eyes, insofar as they were capable of

glistening, glistened. "They were the immortals," he said reverently.

"Well, not altogether," I said. "Two of them aren't dead yet. Anyhow, there they were, Academy Award winners all, but their current productions, as it happened, were bombs. Every man jack of them was covered with flop sweat, and you ask why? Because not one—I repeat, not one—had a motif."

"But that's precisely why I needed to see you! I mean so I could like steep myself in the residue, the effluvia, of your experience." He drew a deep breath. "I've decided to make a full-length documentary about jeans."

"Genes?" I asked dubiously. "DNA, mutations, all that stuff?"

"No, no—*Levi's.*" He leaned toward me, his expression rapt. "The symbol of youth's sixties revolt against the crassness and stupidity of the Establishment. How does that grab you for a motif?"

"Fischbyne," I said after a moment's reflection, "every once in a while somebody comes up with an inspiration so dazzling that it leaves one speechless. The last time it happened to me was back in the Golden Age when Hunt (Wild Hunt) Stromberg told me his production plans for *Naughty Marietta,* with Nelson Eddy and Jeanette MacDonald."

His face grew radiant. "You really like it?"

"It's a winner, kid. It's got everything—heart, lungs, liver, and twice the box-office appeal of *Chain Saw Massacre* and *Death Trap.* Furthermore, you can bankroll the whole production with one phone call—to Levi Strauss in San Francisco. They'll flip. Think of the pants potential."

His face stopped radiating. "Wait a minute," he objected. "You and I seem to be on two different wavelengths—the commercial and the artistic. It's true I've only made a couple of films, but both of them lost money, and I don't intend to compromise now."

"Holy cow, no—never compromise!" I enjoined him. "But don't you want—I mean, would it hurt if your picture got back its negative cost?"

"I'd much rather it didn't, so I can go on being a young film-maker," he said earnestly. "Now, the technique I have in mind occurred to me while I was watching some glue being melted. It would be a slow, dreamy montage of abstract shapes endlessly weaving in and out, underscored by sitar music and gourds."

"The jeans," I ventured, seeking to lure him back to reality. "I'm trying to envisage how they'd fit in with the abstractions."

"Well, I'm not sure whether I'll show them at all. They might detract from the purity of the concept."

"Yes, it might easily be a false note. Tell me, will the audience —assuming there *will* be an audience—be able to grasp the motif?"

"Actually," returned Fischbyne, "I'd much prefer if they didn't. You see," he explained, "in a sense, a director like me is a magician. I enchant and delight the public, but I also mystify them. And I do that by withholding little things from them— motifs, bits of plot, et cetera. But I also give them something in return—the feeling that we're communicating, that through the witchery of the lens we've established a dialogue."

"A *viable* dialogue," I corrected, and arose. "Well, Strobe, if I may address you by your first name—What *is* your first name, by the way?"

He reddened. "Stanley. I haven't used it since I turned pro-fessional."

"A good name, my boy. Wear it proudly, for it belonged to one who, aided by a merciful God and infinite courage, won eternal renown on the Dark Continent—"

Simultaneously, with a report that clove the skull, a rock group exploded on the jukebox, blotting out the remainder of my sentence, which ran: "—and let us hope, Stanley, that one day the same merciful God will wrest the megaphone from your hands and consign you to the shipping department, where you belong." Fischbyne, meanwhile, was mouthing something in-audible that I took to be gratitude, but I wouldn't bet on it. Could be he was reviling me.

Thus, then, our brief and seemingly fruitless colloquy in bohemia. Nevertheless, it had an unexpected sequel. Six weeks afterward, at Lindos, on the isle of Rhodes, I received the following cable:

"PROFOUND THANKS INVALUABLE ADVICE NEPHEW STOP STANLEY FORMERLY STROBE ABANDONING FILM CAREER STOP COMMENCING MERCANTILE DITTO KORVETTES SHIPPING ROOM MONDAY EXCELLENT SALARY STOP WHOLE FAMILY ECSTATIC BLESSINGS AND BON VOYAGE ROLAND PORTFOLIO."

All Precincts Beware—
Paper Tigress Loose!

Saturnine, tweedy Gabe Hammerschlag, head of the N.Y.P.D.'s Confidence Detail, struck a match on his desk top and, sucking the flame into the bowl of his pipe, eyed me meditatively. Gabe and I had known each other ever since 1953, when I had helped him straighten out a rather nasty copyright mess among the Kachins of Northern Burma, and I knew that when Hammerschlag sucked flames meditatively into his pipe bowl the unexpected could be expected.

"Sir Herbert Lopretni phoned me from London the other night," he said abruptly. "His name mean anything to you?"

I frowned, the loose skin on my forehead corrugating into parallel ridges. "There are those who think it could stand for Interpol spelled backward."

"I wouldn't know about that." His face was a mask. "But this I do know—we've a crisis on our hands, and it's going to take a pretty special type of chap to sort it out. Passive to the point of stupidity on the surface, yet keen as mustard underneath. Only one man in this city answers to that description."

Despite myself, I blushed at the compliment. "Why, thanks, Gabe."

"Good. Then here's the drill—we're going to use you for bait, as a decoy. The way shikaris stake out a goat in India."

"Oh? And just who is the tiger, pray?"

"Say, rather, the tigress. The wiliest, most dangerous feline ever to stalk the world of wholesale stationery."

"That's a metaphor of some kind, I gather."

"No, I'm being quite literal." He produced a file from his desk and opened it. "Early last May, ten men were convicted in London's Central Criminal Court of participating in a huge carbon-paper fraud. Immense quantities of the paper were sold at inflated prices to the purchasing agents of a number of British companies. Get the picture? Then let me read you the Crown prosecutor's account of how the gang operated, as reported in the London *Times*: 'Company buyers, known as "dupes," were bribed with champagne, cigarettes, or cash and then threatened with exposure to their employers once they succumbed to the stationery salesmen, he [the Crown prosecutor] said. . . . An Exeter store, Bobby and Company, paid out £70,000 in 18 months and was invoiced with 3,750,000 sheets of carbon, enough to last the typists 3,000 years, he added. The Northern Ireland firm of Ulster Carpet Mills were invoiced with enough for 400 years and the Coöperative Society in Bangor, North Wales, got 438,900 sheets, enough for 290 years.' "

"But the perpetrators—or paper traitors, so to speak—were caught," I objected. "Whence hence this tigress of yours?"

"Precisely—that's what has baffled the police of two continents, causing us to scratch our polls in bewilderment. Obviously, these men were puppets, fuschers, boneheads. Behind them there had to be a cold, diabolic intelligence akin to that of a Fu Manchu or a Professor Moriarty—housed, as Lopretni and I believe, in the body of a supremely beautiful woman. From Cesare Lombroso to Craig Kennedy the Scientific Detective, sleuthdom has clung to one cardinal principle—*Cherchez la femme.*"

"Then are you implying," I queried, "that somewhere in this puzzling affair there lurks a she-devil, maddened by who can say what dark neurotic compulsion, dedicated to undermining the very foundations of stationery as we know it today?"

"Yes, yes," he said fretfully. "I just *told* you that. Well, it only remains to add that somehow Mademoiselle L'Inconnue—her name is unimportant; she changes it at will—has either slipped through the immigration net into Manhattan or not. Where or when she will strike nobody can predict, nor is a description worth a plugged nickel, she being a past-master at disguise." He dusted his hands. "Look, go hang around a few stationery stores and see what happens. Right now I got a million other things on my mind."

"Gabe," I pleaded. "Give me at least a hint of what to anticipate—"

"For Chrissake, am I a magician?" he shouted. "I sit here day after day in this crummy office worrying how to get up the rent, the insurance, my alimony payments, and now I'm supposed to be Mr. Answer Man! Who Killed Cock Robin? Who was the Dark Lady of the Sonnets? What was S. S. Van Dine's real name?" He beat clenched fists on his blotter. "I can't stand it, I tell you! I'm up to here!"

"O.K., Gabe, O.K.," I placated him softly, sidling toward the door. "I'll get back to you the second anything jells."

A chill gust sent fragments of newspaper eddying up the gutters of East Twenty-third Street as, weary in spirit, I crossed Lexington Avenue and headed toward Third. Since nine that morning, I had doggedly checked every stationer's along lower Madison and Park Avenues, hoping to espy one woman resembling the criminal genius Hammerschlag had postulated. All their salespersons, without exception, tall or short, slim or fat, had proved to be vapid boobies devoid of any sinister charisma, and now, with only one such store in the district left to investigate, instinct whispered that I might be pursuing a phantom. Approaching the shop, I cast a mechanical glance over its windowful of cut-rate diaries, staplers, pencil sharpeners, and ball-points, and peered past them into the interior. In the next instant, I stood transfixed.

What was Faye Dunaway doing in this unlikely place? And *working* in it, moreover, judging from the delft-blue smock she was clad in. She must be involved in a film or an upcoming television special. . . . Still, where were the cameras, the generator, the technicians? Perhaps in the rear, where I couldn't see too clearly, a director with cordovan leggings, reversed tweed cap, and a suède whistle was outlining the shot. Simultaneously, another possibility presented itself. Back in the days when she was a struggling drama student, had she worked here part time, returning today out of sentimentality to schmooze with the boss? But in that case a Camargue or a Fleetwood Cadillac befitting a star would be idling at the curb. . . . The devil take these hypotheses; chance had thrown a mystery in my path, and it was incumbent on me to sniff it out.

No sooner was I inside the door than I realized my identification was faulty—the plate glass, ashimmer with worry birds and assorted novelties, had distorted the lady's image. Rather than Dunaway, this was another cupcake, equally a goddess. The face was a pastiche combining elements of Corinne Griffith, Olga Baclanova, and Mary Astor; the smock concealed a figure, lithe as that of a great tawny cat, that owed nothing to Lauren Bacall or Lilyan Tashman. By that I mean she was rangy. Withal, so husky was her contralto voice, so reminiscent its lisp of Kay Francis, that when she asked me what I wanted shivers coursed up and down my spine.

"Why—er—catch pads," I faltered. "You know, for scratching on."

"For scratching?" she repeated. Her hazel-brown eyes clouded in perplexity. "But this isn't a drugstore. Do you speak English?"

I stared at her wordless, wondering why her eyes evoked hazelnuts, except that they reminded me of October and woodsmoke and lovers wandering hand in hand down forest lanes. Poignancy welled up in my throat, and, with an effort, I recovered my tongue.

"Sure, I'm native-born," I said defensively. "You see, I'm by profession a writer. I'm always jotting down thoughts, ideas, *aperçus*—fleeting impressions and insights. So this is why I'm needing pads rather than match covers and pieces of Kleenex. You can understand that, can't you?" I implored.

"You're a real *writer?*" Her eyes widened in admiration—a phenomenon I could hardly credit, for already they were wider than even Joan Blondell's. "We don't get many in this neighborhood. They're mostly west of here, over around the Hotel Chelsea, but their beards and jeans are scruffy, whereas you— well, you look as though you stepped out of a bandbox." My heart melted. Before I could mutter some self-deprecatory phrase, she had plunged on, dispensing further catnip. "Is that coat genuine Harris Tweed? You must have got it in England; doubtless you have all your clothes made in Saville Row. . . ."

Divine as I found the harmony of her words, I couldn't help but notice a blue-jowled citizen in shirtsleeves behind the counter, a cigar clenched in his teeth, regarding me with suspicion. "The scratch pads, Miss," I said nervously. "You're stocking them in various sizes?"

"Oh, yes, indeed. They're on the shelf back there." She preceded me through two narrow aisles packed with office supplies, paused before an assortment in different sizes and colors. "Which did you have in mind?"

"This little one with the gray cover—how much is that?"

"Fifteen cents. A dozen in a package for a dollar sixty-seven."

"I don't need a package. I just want one, for like scribbling down an apothegm or so that pops into my mind."

"But supposing more than one apothegm pops in—five or six?" In the constricted area of the aisle, forced into proximity as we were by ledgers, ring binders, and jars of mucilage, her scent of Mitsouko and those extraordinary eyes were creating a hypnotic effect on me. "You'd kick yourself if you ran short of paper. Doesn't it make sense to buy a dozen and save thirteen cents on the price?"

"Well, I . . . all right," I said weakly. "I'll take a package. Could you wrap—"

"On the other hand," she pursued, "two packages, at three dollars and seven cents, would be real thrifty, a saving of twenty-seven cents."

"I know, but I can only use—"

"You certainly can use twenty-seven cents—everyone can. As

a matter of fact, the intelligent thing is to buy a gross, ordinarily seventeen dollars and forty-eight cents, but, lucky for you, we're taking inventory and we can let you have it for sixteen fifty-two."

The faint drumming sensation in my ears grew louder and my legs felt incapable of sustaining my weight. "Lady, who's got space for a gross? I'm living in two small furnished rooms. It's like the Collyer brothers' in there!"

"But space is never a problem," she whispered, though here, with lips a hairbreadth from mine, it was rapidly becoming one. "If, for example, we invoiced you for a carload, we could keep it for you on a siding. The pads would be only six cents a unit, and they'd last you two thousand years. So you will—take a chance!"

"I can't—I mustn't," I choked. 'I'll think it over—I'll give you a commitment in thirty days—"

"Goodness me, it's lunchtime!" she broke in, with a surprised glance at her watch. "Listen, there's a cute little tearoom around the corner where we can discuss the whole thing, away from all this noise and frenzy. Come on, it's my treat."

While our present locale struck me as more suitable for a business talk, I deemed it graceless to cavil and, albeit reluctantly, acquiesced. The Persian Kitten, when we arrived there, sported a façade more bar than tearoom, with a tiny slit window and a heavily armored door. Its interior, lit by a few amber bulbs, was so crepuscular that I at once fell over a rock-maple chair and skinned my knee. Fearing it might lead to tetanus if neglected, I strove to examine it by the light of a match, but my companion pooh-poohed the mishap and bade me choose an apéritif. After consideration, I agreed to a little white wine and seltzer.

"Rats, you sound like a sorority pledge at Sophie Newcomb College," she said contemptuously, and called off into the gloom, "Hey, Paddy, crack a bottle of Dom Pérignon—and put aside a couple more for my guest to take home." She turned back to me. "How are you fixed for cigarettes? . . . Only that pack? Paddy, are you there? Send out to the smoke shop for three cartons of straw-tipped Melachrinos." She pulled her chair closer. "Why, your hand's like ice," she said, patting it. "And your teeth are chattering. What's the matter? Don't you trust me?"

Simpleton that I was, I did. It would have been less than human not to, seated there in the cozy darkness with champagne warming my stomach and hands enclasped with so luscious a creature. Yet imperceptibly a nameless terror began to pervade me as her endearments gave way to a brutal, unashamed sales talk.

"What are you—a pantywaist?" she scoffed. "You're going to rest content with a measly carload of scratch pads? Where would the Wizard of Menlo Park have wound up if he'd quit with the prototype electric bulb? Or Haldeman-Julius with the first of his Little Blue Books? I know where you can pick up an entire *warehouse* of memo pads—better still, a whole forest to make them! You could be a greater novelist than Trollope, a bigger paper tycoon than Weyerhaeuser! Here, precious," she raced on, extracting a roll of greenbacks from her stocking, "accept this as an earnest of friendship between the two of us. Not a bribe, mind you—"

Cra-a-ck! Suddenly the rear door of The Persian Kitten buckled under the hammer blows of Gabe Hammerschlag's emergency squad, and forthwith ensued a melee punctuated by harsh commands to freeze and the crunch of fists on bone. When it subsided, and the squad members felled by one another, owing to scanty illumination, were hoisted to their feet, Gabe finished manacling my would-be seductress and dispatched her, snarling and unrepentant, to be booked under Section 4-B—vending wholesale without even a retail license.

"A close call, that," he commented, as we quaffed the balance of the wine. "Fortunate for all, the blue-jowled proprietor of that store phoned us your whereabouts so we could intervene in time. Well done, old chap. Thanks to you, local and international stationery can sleep peacefully tonight."

Yes, I thought ruefully, but, try as I might, I could not rid myself of the memory of a pair of hazel-brown eyes. If I was the goat and she the cupcake, why had I denied myself the privilege of a nibble? *Basta!* Hammerschlag's characterization was only half right. Passive to the point of stupidity on the surface I was, but dull as a hoe underneath.

Methinks the Lady Doth Propel Too Much

What red-blooded male of my generation, unless he has spent his life immured in a Nepalese monastery or footloose in the Empty Quarter of Arabia, has not heard of toothsome Alma Mahler? For those who haven't, Alma Mahler was the foremost sex kitten in Central Europe in the first quarter of the twentieth century, a lady whose fame rested on the fact that four headliners rested on her—the eminent composer; the poet and novelist Franz Werfel; Walter Gropius, of the Bauhaus; and Oskar Kokoschka, the painter. She was, successively, if not in that order, the wife and/or sweet patootie of the quartet, and the veracity of the anecdote that follows was sworn to me by a stateless Bukovinan in Rhodes. And for anyone who has ever known a stateless Bukovinan in Rhodes, nuf sed.

It appears that, in the period she was rooming with Kokoschka, Alma became infatuated with a celebrity in the world of science—a biologist named Pitzel. Physically, Professor Pitzel was unimpressive; a troglodyte just over four feet in height, he was myopic, ill-favored, and snappish, but he was engaged in a wondrous experiment. From deep in Lake Titicaca, on the Peru-Bolivia border, he had retrieved a family of salamanders, creatures that had been sightless for two hundred million years, and was grafting eyes onto them. Day after day, Alma hung around his laboratory breathlessly watching the

Professor amid his retorts and Bunsen burners, and at nightfall she would hustle back to rhapsodize to Kokoschka.

"A genius, Oskar—*ganz unglaublich!*" she bleated. "While you stand here schmiering on canvas, over there is a wizard creating miracles. Professor Pitzel . . . Professor Pitzel . . ."

Naturally enough, her bedfellow's amour-propre was not increased by such hosannas, and he sometimes became so jealous that he broke his maulstick over his knee. The episode reached its climax on the afternoon she raced into his studio with her face aglow.

"Oskar, Oskar!" she exulted. "Glorious news! Today, for the first time in two hundred million years, the salamanders opened their eyes!"

"Yes," said Kokoschka through his teeth, "and the first thing they saw was Professor Pitzel."

The story obtruded itself on my memory last year, when I read about someone who seemed to have accomplished a feat quite as remarkable as the Professor's. "A Brooklyn woman," the *Times* announced in its weekly tally of recent inventions, "has invented a suit designed to convert a female swimmer into a mermaid. Mrs. Chloe Grilli, a professional pianist, was granted Patent 3,344,449 this week. Her garment covers the body and legs from the waist down, with a pair of fins, or flippers, over the feet. . . . The patent explains that the wearer gets propulsion by kicking and manipulating the fins. It is said that the swimmer can dive gracefully, and on land can maneuver along, caterpillar style." Evidently on the assumption that if the invention flopped a buck could be made elsewhere, the item added, "Mrs. Grilli has written an Off Broadway show, 'The Very Gay Prima Donna,' and hopes to have it produced soon."

No sibyl, not even the most gifted astrologer, could have foretold that Mrs. Grilli's oceanic doodad was fated to touch my life, yet early in July, commencing a fortnight's vacation on Martha's Vineyard, I shortly became aware that complications were in store. The manager of Breinig's Market, where I bought a sizable order of groceries, refused to honor my New York check. I explained I was a longtime visitor to the Island, currently staying in a nearby efficiency that I rented from Herman Moulmein.

"You mean the Herman Mealman who's the mailman?"

"No, Moulmein, as in Kipling. You know, the old Moulmein pagoda in 'Mandalay.' "

"What about it?"

"I'm only trying to tell you how the name is spelled. His family have lived here for generations—they made whaling history."

"The one I mean made deadbeat history." The grocer was a leathery old crab, with eyes of pure flint. "We're a cash-and-carry operation, friend. It'll cost you thirty-one dollars and eighty-seven cents cash to carry that bag out of here."

Well, you can't argue with a mentality like that, so I shelled out the money. Moulmein was reading the *Vineyard Gazette* on his piazza when I got home.

"Look, this is a nuisance," I said. "They always took my check up-Island, at Chilmark and Menemsha. Why are they so suspicious down here?"

"Not suspicious, just careful," he said, with a cold little smile. "We get a lot of riffraff in the summer."

I chewed that over, wondering how he classified me, and decided to skip it. "Thing is"—I cleared my throat—"I'm going to run short of cash very soon. Maybe you could vouch for me over at the bank."

His wattles froze as if someone had applied an ice collar to them. "Are you asking me to stand good for your checks?"

"No, it's just that I come from a long line of eccentrics. I like to have a fiver or so in my pocket in case of emergency."

"Then do what I do." He hiked up his sweater. "There's two thousand berries stowed in this money belt at all times. That way, I don't have to go around begging folks to vouch for me."

"I see. Well, I'll get one, in case I ever come back here."

"But keep it a secret from your family," he warned. "I don't even tell my wife. Women gabble."

For someone raised, as I was, in New England and weaned on the works of Joseph C. Lincoln, I had forgotten how salty the natives were. I tried another tack. "By the way, could you recommend a good barber in town?"

Moulmein scratched his nose reflectively. "I could, but I won't," he said finally. "If you complained, he'd probably give me a rotten haircut next time I go in."

"Yes, that makes sense," I agreed. "Hmm. Well, guess I'll drive over to Edgartown and buy a can opener. I *was* going to borrow one locally, but I imagine people are wary about lending them."

The hush that ensued, plus Moulmein's absorption in his paper, confirmed my fears. I went upstairs, parked the groceries, and, assembling the gear I needed for the beach, bore it down to my car. Moulmein had vanished, and, to insure against depredations by the riffraff, had taken his rocker with him.

Unpropitiously as the day had begun, though, an hour later I was in as paradisaical a situation as any mortal could wish for, recumbent in a sheltered nook on the beach between West Tisbury and Chilmark. The sky was cloudless, and zephyrs fanned my brow as I lay there, my head supported by Motley's *The Rise of the Dutch Republic,* watching the majestic combers boom in from Portugal and thinking equally majestic thoughts. Why not gather a few kindred spirits in a poets' commune right here? We could subsist on cranberries and fish cunningly netted from these waters, wax our own batiks, and betweentimes play the lute and recite the georgics that must inevitably spring from such halcyon surroundings. By Jove, what a crackerjack idea! I sat up, overcome by the brilliance of the inspiration. It was then, despite vision dazzled by the noonday sun, that I caught sight of the phenomenon crawling toward me along the shoreline.

She was incontestably female, and she was moving ahead like an inchworm, using elbows for locomotion—her only recourse, inasmuch as her trunk ended in a fishtail. Unable to credit my

senses, I stared at her transfixed, and at last, satisfied that she was
no chimera, approached for a closer look. How to describe her
loveliness? She was rapture personified, a naiad whose olive skin,
blue-black hair, and green eyes would have captivated the most
embittered misogynist, and from the instant her lashes fluttered
upward at me I was hers, body and soul.

"Uh—excuse me, Miss," I stammered. "I hope I'm not being
forward, but who are you?"

"What do you mean who am I?" she demanded pertly.
"Haven't you ever seen a mermaid before?"

"Oh, come on," I retorted. "I wasn't born yesterday. Do you
see any green in my eye?" Then, as the words left my mouth,
I hurried to make amends. "I mean, I see plenty in yours—and
they're very beautiful, may I say—but everyone knows mermaids
are fabled creatures who lure sailors to their doom."

She bridled. "Why, that's hateful—*I* never have. Some of my
best friends are sailors."

"Right, right," I agreed quickly. "Where would we be without them, plowing the deep and reefing the topsails and all? But
what I'm driving at is, can I assist you in any way, me being well
acquainted in these parts and you a stranger? You've evidently
crept a long way, judging from the amount of sand in your
hair."

"Yes, I have." She fingered her locks self-consciously. "Goodness, I must look a perfect fright. You wouldn't happen to have
a comb, would you?"

"Sure, in that grocery bag over yonder. Can you reach it O.K.?
If not, I'll be glad to carry you."

She signified there was nothing wrong with her—a diagnosis
I had already made—and cumbrously wove her way there. I sat
by, munching a Goldenberg Nut Chew while she untangled her
tresses and shook them luxuriously over her shoulders.

"Listen, why don't you pile your hair up in a knot the way
the Gibson girls used to?" I suggested. "You know, in what they
call the *guiche*, or concierge, style. It may be a trifle sexy, but
we older chaps go for it."

Typical of womankind, whether terrestrial or marine, she knew better. "No, it's more becoming around my face. It softens the features."

"Golly, nobody's could be softer than yours," I protested. "You haven't got a wrinkle I can see. Oh, yes, maybe a crow's-foot or two, but that's undoubtedly from the strain of creeping."

"And hunger, too—I'm starved. What is that you're eating?"

"It's a candy bar, invented by a little professor in Central Europe. People had been eating plain chocolate for two hundred million years until he grafted peanuts onto it. Do you care for some?"

"It sounds horrid."

"No, it's quite yummy, in fact. But I suppose you generally subsist on briny foods like plankton and mollusks, what?"

"Yes, and salads. I adore salads—I often make a whole meal off them."

"I shouldn't wonder. These waters around the Vineyard teem with salads. By the way," I broke off, "we haven't introduced ourselves properly, have we? My name's Henry Knifesmith. It used to be Hans Messerschmitt in the old country, but we Anglicized it when we came over."

Her eyes clouded with suspicion. "I think you're pulling my tail."

"No, really. When my brother Fritz and I were boys—we were known as Hans und Fritz—we were two little devils, always up to some mischief. We used to tease our father, der Captain, unmercifully, and as for his best friend, the Inspector, he used to cry *'Was ist los?'* and jump up and down on his tall beaver hat."

"But why are you telling me all this?" she asked, echoing a line I recalled having heard in a play.

"Oh, I don't know—I guess it's because I feel so drawn to you." Assuming a shy expression compounded of equal parts of James Stewart and Glenn Hunter, I dug my toe awkwardly in the hot sand. "Gee, Miss, you're the most beautiful lady I ever saw. I'm crazy about you, but I know that if I reached out to touch you you'd vanish."

"Listen, Buster." Her face hardened. "If you reached out to

touch me, you'd get a blow from these flukes that would send you reeling. You don't know what strength we mermaids have in our tails."

"Ah, yes, you mermaids." Suddenly my face hardened to twice the rigidity of hers. 'I was just getting around to that. Tell me, did you ever hear of a Mrs. Chloe Grilli, in Brooklyn—a pianist-playwright who invented a suit designed to transform a female swimmer into a mermaid?"

"I—I've no idea what you're talking about." Olive an instant before, her face had gone white.

"Don't play the innocent with me, sister," I said roughly. "You knew all about that suit, *didn't* you? And you lusted for it with every fibre of your being, *didn't* you?" I drove on remorselessly. "And finally you found one at a garage sale, mayhap, or a students' and misfits' clothing store. And you saw in it a way to ensnare the unsuspecting, first borrowing their combs, then graduating to saltwater taffy, shore dinners, joyrides—"

Defenses crumbling like sand castles, she burst into sobs. "We meant no harm," she blubbered. "It was a thoughtless schoolgirl prank, devised between I and others at Miss Madeira's School over a Welsh rabbit in our dorm. Ere I knew what possessed me, I was inching up here from Oak Bluffs, elbows sorely enchafed. Please, please don't squeal on me."

"I have no wish to, my dear," I said generously, and arose. "Good day, and leave us hope this experience will be a salutary lesson in eschewing false plumage. The environment is bleak enough without phony mermaids lousing up the strand."

Moulmein was again seated on his piazza when I returned. He looked up from his paper. "Get your can opener?"

"Well, no, but I saw a very strange thing up-Island."

"What's that?"

"Never mind," I replied, and shut up like a clam. I knew what kind of response I'd get out of him.

Scram! You Made the Pants Too Short

W hen an Englishwoman named Victoria Glendinning—whom I somehow conceive of as a tall, radiant beauty clad in a Laura Ashley dress, and with that marvellous complexion they have over there, no matter how grasping the unions are—sat down a while ago to review a book of photographs called *Lady Ottoline's Album* for *The Times Literary Supplement*, she little dreamt that her first sentence would take the words right out of my mouth. Those words, already masticated to the consistency of Wheatena, read, "Bloomsbury has been over-exposed in the past few years, as the biographies, memoirs and collected letters have rolled off the presses." Man, was that ever British understatement. Nothing, but nothing, has been left unsaid about Virginia and Leonard Woolf, Lytton Strachey, Aldous Huxley, T. S. Eliot, Duncan Grant, Henry Lamb, Dora Carrington, u.s.w. Every reader, chick or child, knew by now what fantasies had stoked their neuroses and tickled their libidos, what subterranean fires lay banked under their imperishable works, who had frolicked with whom in what daisy chains. It was high time, in short, that the gossips stopped beating their gums.

Nonetheless, Mrs. Glendinning saw in *Lady Ottoline's Album* a chance to wring a few more drops of elixir out of these talents and the hostess under whose roof they congregated, and she rolled up her sleeves. A good many of the male celebrities snapped by Lady Ottoline at Garsington, her country house, were apparently chosen as much for their dimples as for their brain power, and there is more than an imputation that she cavorted in the supercales with machos like Bertrand Russell and Augustus John. Mrs. Glendinning girlishly admits to being turned on by Siegfried Sassoon's "dark, nervy, attractive face," Lord David Cecil's "elegant profile," and as for T. S. Eliot, "a sweetness in his face for which one was not prepared." In contrast, she disparages André Gide's "sharp, narrowed eyes . . . long, rather cruel mouth" and shafts him with the icy comment "Besides, he was bald, and one bald intellectual looks much like another." Mrs. Glendinning is nobody to talk about cruelty in mouths, having taken the words out of mine, but such naked prejudice against naked pates verges dangerously on Fascism. Let one whose hair is thinning on top urge restraint, lest she start burning books instead of reviewing them.

As for the chatelaine of Garsington herself, the reviewer's tone alternates between the syrupy and the astringent. "Plain at sixteen, Lady Ottoline was magnificent at twenty," she says in one breath, only to sear her in the next with an allusion to "the jutting chin and what Augustus John called her 'bold baronial nose.'" (Still, this is kinder than if he had called it a bald baronial nose.) An insipid marine view of the noble lady later in life does excite her compassion, but she exculpates her: "There is another surprising picture of Lady Ottoline at the seaside, in a bathing suit, in much the same pose as she assumed in bed [in Venice], but vertical; if it is less alluring, it is probably the bathing suit's fault. Those woolly garments which gave no support to the bosom and terminated at the cruellest point, just above the knee, would have been too much even for Aphrodite." Cruelty in mouths, cruelty in bathing suits—what *is* this with Mrs. Glendinning? I started to get all shivery, like the first time I read the Marquis de Sade.

Truth to tell, not one jot or tittle of the foregoing could possibly be deemed momentous except for a throwaway line near the end of the review. Smack on the heels of a discontinuity about men's wide-brimmed hats, some alterations in W. B. Yeats' physique, and similar trivia comes the sudden pettish demand "And why did E. M. Forster wear his trousers three inches too short?" I fell back into my Barcalounger, utterly flummoxed. For whom were the trousers too short? The elegant company at Garsington? For Mrs. Glendinning? Or for E. M. Forster himself? The longer I thought about it, the more convinced I grew that here was an enigma that hungered for explication. The belletristic role of pants, after all, could not be minimized. It was through a member of this very Bloombury circle that they had achieved poetic significance: T. S. Eliot's "I grow old . . . I grow old . . . I shall wear the bottoms of my trousers rolled." And, more recently, what about James Joyce's legal involvement with a pair of pants in Tom Stoppard's *Travesties*? Yes, by George, this was literary research tailor-made, you might say, for me, but it posed a dilemma. Where could I promote the funds to back me in such a work of scholarship?

The answer—a dismal one—was speedily forthcoming. Replying to my application, an official of the National Endowment for the Humanities wrote that he remembered me as the recipient of a Litt.D. he had conferred when president of Brown University. "As I recall, however, you still lack three points in the freshman trigonometry you flunked in 1921," he reminded me. "You ought to do something about that—people are talking. . . . *Re* your inquiry into Forster's pants, wd. say that chances for a handout don't seem hopeful. We have a Mt. Holyoke grad overseas sifting Thomas Hood's 'The Song of the Shirt' and a Yalie here digging into Senator Vest's 'Tribute to a Dog.' Consensus is your project wd. put too much emphasis on matters sartorial." The National Institute of Arts and Letters took a stronger line. "A fine one you are to beg for a subsidy," snarled the Award Committee for Literature in its letter. "Investigate your own pants, you schnorrer. Your pockets are full of the stamps you peel off from our prepaid envelopes. A trolley car should grow in your stomach." The situation, in a word, was bleak. There was no patroness like Joyce's Harriet Shaw Weaver to put the bite on, and whatever rich society woman I approached would, I knew, inevitably exact payment too horrid to contemplate. The prospect of fluttering like a tiny wounded bird in their boudoirs sickened me, so I chose the only other alternative. I put up my passbook as collateral with the Usurers & Defalcators National and bought myself an economy flight to London.

The first order of business, clearly, was to determine what had become of Forster's wardrobe after his demise, and I hastened to King's College at Cambridge, where he had resided. Though most gracious, the warden was unable to aid me, but I did elicit that the writer's former servitor, one Fred Pauncefoot, was still extant and working at a fruiterer's in Petty Cury Street. Thither I repaired and found him, a wrinkled oldster, polishing a tray of pippins. Over a pint of bitter at the corner pub, I conveyed the nature of my quest.

"Aye, his bags," Pauncefoot quavered. "Well, now, that's easier said than done. All his cronies and relations were in there at the finish, jabbering away and snatching up mementos. I remember Coleridge took the spoons and Cavafy stole a quilt—"

"Are you quite certain of that, sir? Coleridge died in 1834 and Cavafy left England almost a hundred years ago."

"Ach, who can remember their names, the spongers?" he said fretfully. "Anyhow, there wasn't a drop of port left when they cleared off. The carpets and the andirons—let me see—oh, yes, they went to Sledgehammer's, the furniture people."

"But his clothes, his suits, I said impatiently. "What happened to them? Did he leave them to anyone?"

Pauncefoot stared at me. "How could he? He was dead at the time."

"No, no, *before*." I signalled for another pint of bitter to jog his memory. "Try to think—when was the last time you saw them?"

"Why, when Goldberg put them in the van. . . . Goldberg. You mean to say you don't know Goldberg?"

His incredulity that I didn't stunned him, or maybe it was the

bitter, but I finally wormed out the information that the afore-
said's gentlemen's resale shop had acquired the clothing.

Half an hour later, thanks to my powers of persuasion,
Goldberg and I were seated in a café next to his store. Actually,
my powers of persuasion had little to do with it. Business, he
confided to me, was rotten.

"Sure I remember what I bought from the estate," he said,
sipping his glass of lemon tea. "Two sports coats, a herringbone
and a pin-check, and three pairs of slacks. The rest they gave
to charity. The coats and two pants I sold to a student from
Nigeria."

"Did you get his address?"

"In Nigeria? Why should I get his address in Nigeria? He
paid cash."

"O.K., then what about the third pair of slacks? You wouldn't
still have them, by any chance?"

"What do you think I have there—a museum? No, those a
lady took. A couple in an Aston Martin—tourists."

"You mean a woman bought the garment for herself?"

"Of course. We sell girls, old ladies, everybody. She tried
them on and they were too short, but she said she would make
alterations."

I reacted as if to a blow in the solar plexus. Could the purchaser have been a certain reviewer for *The Times Literary
Supplement*—a tall, radiant beauty in a Laura Ashley dress?
"Look, Mr. Goldberg, this is important. I'm a detective—a
private eye—and this may be a vital clue. What did she look
like?"

"Who knows?" He shrugged. "A young woman, pale, in a
Victorian schmotta. With long hair and those aviator glasses
they all wear."

Victoria—that was Glendinning's Christian name. I was on
the right track. "Was she tall, would you say? With that
marvellous English skin?"

"Tall, yes. The skin—I didn't notice where it came from. The
man with her, the driver of the Aston Martin, had a red beard."

I nodded. "I know—the kind that conceals a weak chin. Did

you have the feeling they were from London? I don't suppose you copied down their license number?"

"Listen, my friend," he said with dignity. "That only happens in *Kojak*, on the telly. I'm conducting here a gents' resale business."

"To be sure, Mr. Goldberg," I soothed him. "I wasn't implying you were snoopy. Er—one more thing. Did the jackets contain a label of any kind—some bespoke tailor's in Savile Row—whereby they could be traced?"

"No, strictly off-the-peg merchandise—Austin Reed, or one of those other chains." He tapped his forehead. "A brilliant head, Mr. Forster, but a Beau Brummell he was not."

Checkmate. I had reached a dead end, and, what was worse, had plainly aroused the dealer's suspicion. For all I knew, he might tattle to the police and create untold embarrassment, so I decided to transfer my search to London. Someone at Forster's publisher's there, Edward Arnold, was bound to recall details of his attire. In any case, they would certainly welcome an effort to restore lustre to his image. The very next morning, over elevenses outside a snack shop in South Kensington's Bute Street, I hit on a better scheme: the agony column of the London *Times*. Unfolding a serviette, I began constructing an advert for the purchaser of the third set of slacks. "Information Wanted. Will tall, smashing bird owning trousers acquired Cambridge circa 1970 please contact . . ." No, that was too static. I must galvanize readers, excite public attention. "Missing—E. M. Forster's Pants!" I trumpeted. "American collector, scholar, Litt.D., urgently requires whereabouts—"

The screech of automobile tires braking to a halt petrified me, and I spun around. A scant twenty yards away, in the Old Brompton Road, a silvery Aston Martin piloted by a girl in aviator goggles had paused at a light. So striking was her resemblance to the person I had imagined that I shot out of my chair and raced toward the intersection. Just as I neared it, the traffic surged onward, but, blessedly, a cab headed in the same direction materialized, and shouting "Follow that car!," I leaped inside. Away we whizzed past the V. & A. and the

Brompton Oratory, into the turbulence of Knightsbridge, through the underpass at Hyde Park Corner, and along Piccadilly, alternately sighting and losing the fair scorcher. When her vehicle swept north from Leicester Square up the Charing Cross Road, I was ready to abandon the chase, but by then my jehu had concluded I was a member of the Special Branch and held to the trail like a bulldog. Careering wildly around St. Pancras Station, we hurtled through Camden Town and within minutes were ascending the hilltop maze of streets in N.W. 5. Finally, in the upper reaches of the Dartmouth Park Road, the Aston Martin pulled up at a semi-detached villa, rich in curlicues, of the type immortalized by Osbert Lancaster. From a discreet vantage point, I saw with exultation that my quarry, clad in trousers and roll-neck sweater, was seemingly unaware of our presence. The moment she was indoors, I paid off my cabby and rang the bell.

A bulky, fortyish party whose red beard obviously concealed a weak chin answered the door.

"Look here, do forgive this unwarranted intrusion, but I'd appreciate a word with the young lady who just came in here. It's a matter of the highest importance, I assure you."

"Oh?" He was definitely a hollow man; I knew who wore the pants in this household. "May I ask who you are?"

"Professor Gideon Titmarsh, of Rexall College, in Ohio."

He hesitated, motioned me in. "She's changing, but she'll be down in a minute."

I followed him into a tiny, disordered living room.

"Join me in a sherry?"

I declined, and while he busied himself with his drink studied my plan of action. Useless to employ subterfuge or duplicity; I would be open, forthright, gusty, a contrast to this shuttered room.

After a few moments, footsteps sounded on the stair and the lady appeared. She was a lulu, a peachamaroot, and if her figure was less opulent than the Jersey Lily's, my standards were less rigorous than the late monarch's. And whoever had designed the dress, Laura Ashley or Pablo Picasso, sure knew how to make women look willowy.

I arose and sprang to the attack at once. "Pray, let us dispense with formalities, Madam. The trousers you had on a moment ago—are you aware they belonged to E. M. Forster?"

"Indeed." Not a trace of emotion ruffled her perfect composure. "I was under the impression they had no previous history."

"Didn't Goldberg tell you?"

"Alas, Goldberg tells me nothing."

"He never intimated that they were used by the author of *Howards End, A Passage to India, Two Cheers for Democracy,* and *Aspects of the Novel?*"

"Not even by word or gesture."

"Yet knowing you were in a gentlemen's resale shop, a stone's throw from where he had composed those works, the idea never occurred to you?"

"I suppose I was a blind little fool."

"Excuse me," I said coldly. "I did not come here to discuss your deficiencies. Perhaps it would save time if you handed over the pants."

"For what purpose?"

"So I can measure them. I quite realize they were altered, but the old stitch marks should reveal their original length."

"And if I were to refuse?"

"I should be compelled to demand of the authorities that you submit forcibly."

"Just one moment, please." She drew herself up. "Do you imply that I'm harboring or otherwise withholding someone else's property?"

"You and Victoria Glendinning," I said aggrievedly. "You put words in my mouth and she takes them out. All I meant was, if you haven't got the pants, where are they?"

Her answer was as upsetting as it was unexpected. She turned to her red-bearded companion. "He's the one, all right, Vivyan. I'd recognize his voice anywhere."

"Well done, Gillian." He stepped forward, his fists doubled menacingly. "So you're the blackguard who's been making obscene phone calls to my wife and pursuing her in cabs."

"Hold on, my dear sir—"

"And now you have the impudence to storm in here and accuse her of being a transvestite. I ought to thrash you within an inch of your life. What do you have to say for yourself before I hand you over to the police?"

Well, dog my cats, I don't mind telling you I was pretty frightened, but I said it as best I could—told them the whole story—and you know what happened? By the time I finished, they were nodding sympathetically and circulating the sherry. And all of a sudden the most extraordinary coincidence emerged. It turned out that Vivyan's uncle, who'd been a don at Cambridge in Forster's time, was at White's Club at that very moment. They rang him up, roused him out of his drunken stupor, and we all met for lunch at the Connaught. And he told us that once, during the May Bumps, he had borrowed a pair of trousers from Forster, since the two men were the same size, and they fitted him perfectly, breaking just over the shoes—which, I hope, forever disposes of that balderdash about their being three inches too short. So then, to round things off, we signed Victoria Glendinning's name to the luncheon check, in care of *The Times Literary Supplement*. Perhaps that will teach her to keep mum on matters she knows nothing about.

Meanness Rising from the Suds

I used to pride myself on being impervious to the sentimentalities of soap opera, but when that loveliest of English actresses, Rachel Gurney, of *Upstairs, Downstairs*, perished on the *Titanic*, I wept so convulsively and developed such anorexia that I had to be force-fed. Hovering between life and death for weeks, I sat in a Bath chair on the great dappled lawns of my country house with my favorite collie at my feet and an alienist, until one of them—I can't recall which— recommended that I watch a few other soaps to palliate my anguish. So I did; I watched *Another World, Days of Our Lives, As the World Turns,* and *Somerset,* and in less time than you could say "Dr. Gregory Zilboorg" I was whole again. Compared to the torment their characters underwent, Rachel's fate was a piece of cake.

I usually avoid such personal revelations, reserving them for my diary and a few copies for friends, but not long ago a paragraph on this subject, in a periodical called *American Film*, horrified me anew. It said that *True* had examined the treatment of men in daytime soap opera and recoiled in shocked indignity. "Shows like 'Another World,' " it complained, "portrayed men as 'gutless and/or villainous boobs.' Moreover, [*True*] found that most male characters on daytime serials suffer from something, and listed the embarrassments that are visited on the stronger sex: 'sterility, stupidity, amnesia, alcoholism, impotence, night sweats, acne, acrophobia, senility, insecurity, and outright lunacy.' " The item continues, "An editor of a soap opera newsletter told *True* that some actors have quit in protest at the 'shambling fools' their characters were reduced to. Worse, some even found their characters so emasculated that their offscreen sex life was affected."

Hardly able to credit the evidence of my eyes, I swiftly dug up the relevant issue of *True* for confirmation. Every word was gospel. One actor, John Colenback, who has played Dr. Dan Stewart in *As the World Turns* for many years, charged, "The writers I worked with always managed to turn the men on the show into either evil or totally weak characters who were manipulated by women. . . . I was trapped in an extremely paranoid position. I was really vicious when I was working at the hospital, screaming at the nurses and patients like a little Hitler. But at home I had to be the biggest of boobs, pushed around unmercifully by my wife and my mother." (And, judging from that adverb, Colenback's travail also fractured his English.) Furthermore, *True* pointed out, these shows were not alone in their castrating complex, and gave more examples of male *faiblesse* gleaned from *Days of Our Lives*: "A man turns out to be the father of his brother's child. A husband ruins his wife's career by refusing to let her sing in public. . . . A man shaves off his mustache because a girl tells him that she doesn't trust men with face hair." All of them, I was forced to acknowledge, were unspeakable bounders—the husband in particular. Rather than wicked, actually he was a dolt. The craftier way to ruin his wife's career would have been to *compel* her to sing in public.

The second dent of soap opera on my consciousness had barely faded to a purplish bruise when out of left field came another—this time, though, more in the nature of a soft nudge. A ravishing friend of mine who, by a coincidence, had won her acting spurs on *Another World* and was now starred in a network show called *Millionaire Pauper* rang me me up one evening from the Coast. Not for nothing had Kathleen been called the Zuleika Dobson of Hofstra University; in addition to green eyes, honey-colored hair, and a figure that capsized the senses, she had a brain stored with more knowledge than

Chambers's Encyclopædia and a gaiety unequalled since Carole Lombard's. But tonight she was in a sombre mood. "Look, baby, I've got to come up for air," she confided. "I'm skying into town for a couple of nights. Do you know a real person that a person could spend an evening with—not a chauvinist pig or a garter-snapper?"

I tried to think of one, and, failing, timidly nominated myself.

There was a curious pause, and a crackling akin to chuckling, as though we were disconnected. Then I heard her voice. "You?" she asked dubiously. "Yes, you're sweet. But, frankly, dear, I've always felt there was—how shall I say?—something lacking in you."

I bristled. "You mean that I'm kind of weak? Gutless? A boob?"

"No, just ineffectual—sort of Pre-Raphaelite. A bush-league Dante Gabriel Rossetti, so to speak. You'r not really *evil*, like the men on my show. The trouble with you, darling—"

"Listen, this call is costing you an arm and a leg," I broke in, forgetting that she had reversed the charges. "I'll meet you at '21' tomorrow at eight. No, wait—you don't want to be bothered signing autographs. Let's make it the corner of Fifty-eighth and Fifth, and if I'm late you can look in Bergdorf's windows."

The realization that Kathleen conceived of me as a sheep rankled throughout the night, and by morning I decided to change my image. Fie on the funereal lounge suit from Brooks I had worn hitherto, the discreet neckwear, the bespoke shoes; I would transform myself into a swinger, one of those breezy, jovial loudmouths around the Americana Hotel, and sweep her off her feet. At a quarter to seven, I stood aghast regarding my alter ego in the bathroom mirror. The peacock-blue safari suit, the Tibetan prayer beads encircling my neck were disastrous. All I needed was a little tin can on my head to look like Happy Hooligan. Eyes aplenty popped at the Golden Noodle subsequently as the headwaiter ushered Kathleen and me to our table, but they were riveted on her Celtic beauty rather than on me. Understated my old Brooks number may have been; still, it didn't glow in the dark.

Our faces were greasy with egg rolls and spareribs before I mustered up courage to pose the question gnawing at my subconscious. "Kathie," I demanded, "why do you women in soap opera detest my sex?"

"Hate your sex?" The widened eyes turned on me were as lambent as a jaguar's. "My dear, you talk like a sausage. We don't at all."

"You do, you do!" I drummed my fists on the table. "We're always being portrayed as drunkards and eunuchs and fatheads —greedy, lascivious morons without one redeeming virtue."

"But you *are* swine, you can't deny," she said, palms outspread. "Look at Verdun, the Huguenot massacre, the annual statistics on rape."

"And women are angels, I suppose," I retorted. "What about Messalina knocking off her lovers? And Catherine of Russia, Madame Defarge, and Lizzie Borden?"

"Oh, we've had a few hotheads, sure, but if you dig into it, you'll find men were usually to blame. Remember the breakfast Andrew Borden had served up that blazing Fall River morning? Warmed-over mutton soup, leftover mutton, and bananas. No wonder the poor thing went berserk."

"Don't try to squirm out of it," I said roughly. "You and your ilk are helping to perpetrate a lie. How can you accept money for blackening the opposite gender?"

"Well, money is the only thing they give us. I guess it's better than nothing."

"Really. I'm surprised you can sleep nights with that on your conscience."

"I did have trouble at first, until I switched to Compoz. You should, too—it's great for the kind of indignation you're suffering from." She shovelled in a second helping of subgum chow mein with water chestnuts. Typical feminine behavior. They eat a spoonful of yogurt when they're alone, but when you're

buying, man, it's like Thanksgiving. "Now, shape up, honey—
you know better than to bad-mouth my profession. We just
speak the words you writers give us."

"Then we're traitors to our sex," I snapped. "We ought to be
horsewhipped for maligning ourselves."

"Hyperbole," Kathleen dismissed. "Those scribes out there are
merely using soap opera as a confessional. Believe me, I speak
from experience—I lived with one a couple of months last year.
He was a gorgeous animal. Body by Mark Spitz, hair like the
raven's wing, pearly teeth, Byronic profile; the man was a
veritable collage. And clever, too—not a speck of talent, but he
knew exactly whose work to plagiarize. So we're in paradise as
envisioned nowadays by Erica Jong—though, between you and
me, I was brought up on Andrew Lang's *Orange Fairy Book*
and I like to do a little sewing betweentimes."

"What ever attracted you to a bullock like that?" I asked,
repressing a shudder. "Sheer physical perfection is abhorrent to
me. Lacking nobility of mind, love is a barrel without hoops."

"You don't say," she commented. "Would you mind dis-
engaging your foot from mine? There, that's better. . . . Well,
one day I was seated in front of my checkbook, as Sir Arthur
Sullivan's song has it, weary and ill at ease. Not only did it not
balance but, chancing to glance through the cancelled checks, I
discovered that, unbeknownst to me, I was supporting a household in Redondo Beach. I taxed Wolf, my lover, with it, and
learned the place was tenanted by an orphan—a wistful, flaxen-
haired call girl to whom, out of compassion, he had also given
a charge account at I. Magnin."

"Whereupon I imagine you sent him packing."

"Yes, in my white Mercedes 450-SEL, which, blinded by
tears of remorse, he drove into a stanchion on the San Diego
Freeway. The shock to his psyche might have been irreparable,
except that he embodied our idyll in his soap opera and then
wrote it off as a deductible business expense."

"Kathleen mavourneen." I reached over and took her hand—
the one that was not busy spooning up water chestnuts. "How

can you allow yourself to be endlessly exploited by such parasites, trapped in an environment so alien to you? Need I remind you that with each passing day you grow older?"

"Oh, remind me, do," she begged. "That's why I flew three thousand miles—to be warned I was becoming a raddled old crone."

"Well, it isn't too apparent yet," I comforted her. "And anyway there are lots of old-crone parts you'll be able to play. No, what I'm trying to convey is that however stupid or clumsy your past has been, I'm big enough to overlook it."

"Then nothing else matters," she said warmly. "As long as you think I'm straight and clean and fine—"

"I didn't say that," I interrupted. "Let me finish. Now, I'm not very rich in this world's goods, but I know where there's a tiny cabin in a bee-loud glade just large enough for two. Can you guess what I see there?"

Like so many of your Hibernian persuasion, Kathleen is more than a bit psychic, and, after a moment's reflection, she told me. She saw herself bent over a washtub humming contentedly as several chubby youngsters played around her knees and I sat indoors writing paperbacks that I hoped to sell for four hundred thousand each so as to put meat on the table.

"Yes, yes, go on," I encouraged. "Is there anything else you want to tell me?"

"Just one thing, lambie," she said, and patted my hand. "Fearing you might become sleepy after these Chinese dinners you consistently feed me, I availed myself of a backup date with a person staying at the Americana."

"Some loudmouth in a safari suit and prayer beads, no doubt," I said, stung to the quick.

She nodded. "Poor in spirit but not in this world's goods—he owns forty-one per cent of the Texas Panhandle. Hence," she said, rising, "that's why I'm rushing off precipitately, because he can't bear to be kept waiting at '21.'" She imprinted a light kiss on my ear and was gone in a rustle of silk.

Temperamentally, I'm an easygoing, philosophical chap stimulated by rejection, as I've often noted in my diary and a few copies for friends, and within a month the entire episode had faded from memory. Then, one afternoon, as I was watching *Millionaire Pauper*, the soap Kathleen appears on, I was taken aback by a new character introduced as comic relief—a bespectacled writer hopelessly besotted with a glamorous young actress. Torn between satyriasis and parsimony, he insists on conducting her to substandard Chinese restaurants, where he fondles her over the less expensive choices on the à la carte menu—but why should I compound the humiliations? The whole thing is a cowardly slur on the masculine sex, and any male voluntarily tuning in on the show should be horsewhipped. Still, don't let me influence you. That's just one viewer's opinion.

Is There a Writer in the House?

$\mathcal{S}$ome fifteen years ago, I began harboring a suspicion that the individual writer as such was obsolescent and would soon become as extinct as Battenberg insertions, Pluto Water, and Ayvad's Water Wings. Behind more and more of the craft, it struck me, there was becoming visible a corps of assistants, catalysts, technicians, and *accoucheurs*, but, at the same time, these incubators, these keepers of the flame who had breathed on the vital spark, were being denied screen credit. My conviction was shortly verified by a 1965 dispatch to The *Philadelphia Inquirer* from the Baltic: "Helsinki, Finland—Kati Kidstina's first book comes off the press this fall. A combination of poetry and prose, it will be dedicated to her mother. Mrs. Kirstina is especially proud, since Kati is only 3 years old." The dedication, clearly, should have been shared with Mrs. Kirstina's obstetrician, who had also helped out. Three years later, a prominent English press figure begrudged a similar debt. Alongside his photograph in the London *Times* was the caption "Charles Douglas Home, Defence Correspondent of *The Times*, is 29. He says he entered journalism with the publication of a story in the January 1944 issue of *Lilliput*. He was five years old at the time and had dictated it to his mother." Again, nary a mention of physician, nanny, or wet nurse. I was about to indite a letter to the World Health Organization, urging its obstetrical members to withhold prenatal care unless their names appeared on title pages, when *The New York Times* carried an account of

an even more flagrant omission: "Ahmedabad, India (AP) —
Three-year-old Surjit Shah has published his first collection of
short stories, entitled 'Black, Black Rain.' The book, dictated to
Surjit's father in the Gujarati language, has been translated into
English by 8-year-old Claudia Kohn."

As if I still needed proof of the growing hypertrophy in
authorship, it was afforded me my last summer in London. Like
many another Briton, a friend of mine there named Max
Waxwing is involved in a multitude of enterprises. A partner in
an art gallery, he conducts a health-food restaurant and a wine
bar, deals in vintage cars, imports cork ice buckets from Portugal,
and sells medieval oak furniture to persons avid for medieval
oak furniture. Months before, he had casually mentioned a
book he was writing about primitive and self-taught painters,
and I asked how it was progressing.

"Ah, very slowly, I'm afraid," he said, downcast. "Half the
time, he just sits there."

"Who does?"

"Why, the word man. The chap who's putting down the text."

"But you said you were writing it."

"So I am. I give him all the gen, and he whips it into shape."

"Oh, I see. It's a collaboration."

He bridled. "Not at all. Everything in the book"—he tapped
his forehead—"originates right here. He doesn't know damn all
about primitive painting."

"Then why do you bother with him?"

"Because that's his profession, man," he said, plainly annoyed
at my stupidity. "You expect me to sit down and type out the
whole thing?"

"Wouldn't it be simpler if you just reeled it off to a secretary?"

Waxwing compressed his lips. "That's *his* job, for Chrissake.
I tell him the facts, and he goes off and dictates it to some
wretched bint he's living with."

"Aha, now I get it." Light dawned. "She's the one does the
writing."

"Well, she or her flatmate—a repulsive little worm from
Zaïre or wherever." He dusted his hands. "At any rate, I'll be

finished with the rough draft in a few days, and then I begin polishing. That's going to take plenty of midnight oil."

So careworn was he already at the prospect that I urged him to husband his strength for only vital changes, and we parted.

Emerging from Crown Passage into Pall Mall a fortnight afterward, I collided with him. His usual natty garb had given way to the broad-brimmed black Stetson affected by W. B. Yeats, together with a waterproof draped impresario style over his shoulders. "Just come from my publishers," he said wanly. "Gad, what a nightmare. I've had to fight like a tiger to keep them from castrating my work."

My heart bled for him, having endured a like travail myself, but he waved aside my condolences. "Philistines, that's all they are," he spat. "You spend hours evolving a phrase, a nuance, and slash goes the blue pencil. I tell you, it's enough to make a chap give up writing."

"Now, stop talking nonsense," I reproved. "Where would Eugène Sue and Irving Wallace and Rod McKuen be today if they'd quit?"

"I guess you're right," he said, brightening. "Well, can't stand here gossiping all day. I'm due at Christina Foyle's literary luncheon and then that four-thirty symposium about the book on the BBC."

"Hold on a second—I'm confused. Your book hasn't come out yet, has it?"

He looked around furtively. "Not officially, but remember the worm from Zaïre I spoke of? Her cousin—brilliant tutor at the University of Leeds—is brushing up the rough spots in the tapes as soon as they finish detoxifying him. There aren't any actual copies so far in the shops, but everyone in Paternoster Row is buzzing about it."

While I cocked my ear dutifully for such sibilance the rest of my stay, I failed to hear any, nor have I since. Soon after arrival in New York, though, I encountered another instance of pullulating creativity. Through a mouthful of food at Downey's, Rebecca Earwig, a press agent I know, disclosed that she and one Mumtaz Mahal were writing a cookbook.

"Not the favorite wife of Shah Jehan?" I asked incredulously. "Honey, she's been dead for three hundred and fifty years."

"No, this one performed in a Bengali dance troupe that was stranded at the Hotel Edison. I and she are penning a book of the favorite recipes of celebs like Olivia de Havilland, Celeste Holm, and Josh Logan, together with their most sparkling show-biz anecdotes."

"Gee, that ought to be a blitzkrieg. How does one go about writing a cookbook?"

"Well, I call up the diverse personalities, and she does the recording."

"On what—palm leaves?"

"Of course not—on a cassette. Then Mumtaz sets up an audition with a publisher."

"You mean she dances while he listens to the recipes?"

"You know," she said, breathing fire, "sometimes you can be a very aggravating person."

"I'm sorry, I expressed myself badly. What you're saying is that you transcribe the tapes—"

"*I* don't transcribe anything," she said haughtily. "My girl Friday handles that kind of thing. When she's through, the result is edited for like grammatical errors and fluffs."

"By you and this Bengali?"

"No, we haven't time. I'm enmeshed with my P.R. work, and she's grading cardamom seeds in a store downtown. There's some cockamamie instructor in the night school at Brandeis revising the script."

"Won't you have to acknowledge indebtedness to him and the secretary for their coöperation?"

"Are you out of your skull?" she snapped. "I and Mumtaz midwifed the idea between us. Nobody can use the recipes or even the jokes without they pay us a fee!"

So incensed was she at my skepticism that she forgot to demand my favorite recipe—upside-down cookies—and, as for the eventual publication party, I stand less chance of being invited than Father Damien's lepers on Molokai.

With mass authorship erupting all over the place, I became fearful lest I, too, be shanghaied into some congeries of the sort, and I kept my guard up. Unfortunately, it was down one morning when a telephone caller identified himself as Adrian Luftmensch, of Honeyfogle House, a firm of publishers outside my ken. Before I could tell him to put an egg in his shoe and beat it, the man was entreating me to lunch with him.

"What is it about? I can't seem to place your organization."

"That so? Just look us up in Dun & Bradstreet," he said, sensing that I would as likely possess the Book of Kells. "But never mind that—just answer me one question. Is one hour of your time worth five hundred thousand dollars?"

"Yes, and I've already wasted a bundle on you. I've got a five-act tragedy in reverse about H. P. Lovecraft on the front burner, so talk fast."

"I can't over the phone, friend. It's too delicate. Listen, where can we meet—The Four Seasons, Lutèce, '21'? No, on second thought, that's dangerous. If we're seen eating together, some columnist might squeal. . . . Wait, I've got it. Do you know Esteban's, a Puerto Rican fast-food shop at Columbus Avenue and a Hundred and Fifth Street?"

After five minutes of senseless wrangling, we compromised on a rathskeller off Vesey Street, of fragrant memory in Horatio Alger's novels. Thither I went, where once honest bootblacks rescued flaxen-haired maidens from runaway steeds, and found Luftmensch, a toothy entrepreneur exuding charm as specious as his Donegal tweeds. The *plat du jour*—rinderbrust with brown mucilage sauce—came with a side order of flattery for my past achievements, foremost among which, declared Luftmensch, were those matchless Potash and Perlmutter stories. Having dissipated the illusion that I was Montague Glass, I enjoined him to state his business.

"Reet," he said. "We heard on the grapevine that not long ago you and someone else succeeded in communicating through the Ouija board with a number of famous deceased authors."

So the news had leaked out. "Well, yes. A colleague and I conversed briefly with Booth Tarkington, Rex Beach, Scott Fitzgerald, and Alexander Woollcott. What of it?"

"What *of* it? Man alive, it's a scientific breakthrough!" He hugged himself in excitement. "But first—are you satisfied that they were the McCoy, the actual bona-fide scribes?"

"Incontestably. A Madame Blavatsky monitored the exchange at their end. She attested to their legitimacy."

"Wow-*ee*!" he crowed. "Do you realize what a sensational book—what a paperback, movie, TV series it could make? This is the biggest thing since Isaac Newton's fall of gravity, the landing on the moon!" His eyes protruded so alarmingly from their sockets that for a moment I feared a syncope. "I can get you a larger advance than Mailer and all those crumb-bums put together!"

Frail vessel that I was, I must confess my heart skipped a beat at his words. It was not the prospect of the riches he held forth, though they would have bought me the leisure, as well as the necessary quills and ink, to complete my great work on Lovecraft. Rather, it was the elation at the acclaim that would accrue for having breached the veil to the hereafter—that is, if I could establish that the planchette we had employed was unaffected by vodka Martinis.

Luftmensch, however, must have construed my hesitation as reluctance, for he whipped out a blank check and scrawled his signature on it. "Here—you want evidence of my good faith? Fill in any amount you like—fifty, a hundred dollars—to bind the deal."

"Slow down, brother." I restored the jar of horseradish he had overturned. "I've got a bunch of commitments to meet—a child's life of Vito Genovese, a history of woodworking among the Amish. I don't know when I could get to this book."

"You won't have to—that's the twisteroo!" he exulted. "My nephew Pincus, a graduate of Pace University, has a part-time job at *The Village Voice* sorting those classified ads for cohabitation. In his free time, he could take down your whole story in shorthand."

"It's not as simple as all that. There's a legal problem. We'd have to get clearances from the departed."

"What are you saying, Mr. Perlmutter? How can a ghost sign a release?"

"I beg your pardon." My voice suddenly turned icy. "Incorporeal, insubstantial, even ectoplasmic these revenants may be, but I consider the term 'ghost' a vulgarism and impermissible."

"Right, right," he chattered. "I didn't mean they were spooks —just that their signatures wouldn't stand up in court."

"Well, that tears it, I guess," I said, rising abruptly. "Doubtless some influential firm, like Harper & Row or Random House, can work out these minutiae. Nice meeting you, Luftmensch."

"Wait, wait. Don't be so hasty." Dew speckled his forehead in the uprush of inspiration. "How about this idea? We plant you and your friend on the Johnny Carson show with the Ouija. You contact these—uh, phantoms, or whatever you call 'em. And right there, with all of America watching, they agree for you to go ahead with the book. Is that legal enough for you—seventeen million witnesses?"

"An ingenious solution," I congratulated him, struggling to keep my temper. "We research the material, endure the agony of creation, possibly suffer the contumely of the critics, only to share the billing and royalties with Johnny Carson and the whole NBC network? Why, you little measle, I've a good mind to give you a biff in the snoot!"

So there we were, scuffling away like two demented roosters, when the door opened and who should come in but Herbert Mitgang, Israel Shenker, and John Leonard, all of the *Times*. God only knows why they had chosen to dine in a dingy fleabag off Vesey Street, unless perchance they were holding an Ochs roast, but, skilled newshawks all, they knew a hot story when they saw one, and they sped to their typewriters. Each wrote his version with no reliance on tipsters, tapes, or legmen, and Luftmensch and I shared equal discredit. Granted the entire episode was sordid from start to finish, still there was nobody without whose help it would never have been written.

As I Was Going to St. Ives, I Met a Man with Seventeen Wives

Now that the more feisty in our midst have left the table and gone off to Plato's Retreat to loosen their inhibitions, perhaps those of us who have trouble staying awake after eleven o'clock would care to loosen their stays and join me in a toast. This year, friends, happens to be the golden anniversary of a spot where nobody had any trouble staying awake after eleven— a *Nachtlokal* called the Parody Club, on Manhattan's West Forty-eighth Street, at which the team of Clayton, Jackson, and Durante burst into glorious flower in 1928. Since its patrons were packed as tightly as sardines, space there was minimal, but in what was left such disparate connoisseurs of the trio as Robert Benchley, Frank Costello, Edmund Wilson, and John Hay Whitney might have been descried rolling on the floor, over-come by mirth. I myself, a raw youth resolved to learn all of Jimmy Durante's routines by heart, was near-bankrupt from attending the club thrice weekly, while my betrothed sat by aghast, dreams of a European honeymoon fading as I cannibal-ized her dowry to pay for the research.

Among the three or four dozen songs and monologues the audience never tired of, like "Jimmy, the Well-Dressed Man," "So I Ups to Him," and "Shipwreck," with its valiant last line, "Pull for the horizon, it's better than nothing," was a short recitative about an occasion when Durante innocently came into conflict with the law. He had been out for a peaceful stroll with his wife and twelve children, he recounted, when a policeman suddenly materialized and took him into custody. Durante was transfixed. "Under arrest, Officer?" he stammered. "What for? I didn't do nothin'!" "None of your lip," the cop retorted. "You must have done *something*, with that crowd follying you."

Much the same suspicion flooded into my mind a while ago about the defendant in a Far Eastern trial reported by the *Times*. Headlined "117-year-old Malaysian Guilty in 'Living out of Wedlock' Case," the story, emanating from Kuala Lumpur, read: "A Moslem religious court has released a 117-year-old Malaysian man on probation after he pleaded guilty to living out of wedlock with a 40-year-old woman. It was his third conviction on the same charge with the same woman, court officials said. The court fined Lebai Omar Bin Datuk Panglima Garang $80 at the hearing yesterday. Lebai Omar described himself as a teacher of 'Silat,' the Malay art of self-defense. He had been married seventeen times previously and divorced all his wives."

On the face of it, it seems improbable that anyone skilled in the art of self-defense could have voluntarily married seventeen women, but doubtless the man was an irrepressible idealist, a matrimonial Audubon doomed to wander aimlessly questing the bluebird of happiness. Still, I reflected, one was forced to admire his doggedness. Unlike such amateurs as Tommy Manville and Artie Shaw, who lost heart after a paltry eight or eleven wives, Lebai Omar gamely pressed on, confident that in the next shower of rice and old shoes he would come up with a winner. In an attempt to gauge the length of his individual marriages, I got out my calculator and estimated that if he had started at the age of thirteen, the average union ran six years. On the other hand, he may have been precocious and begun marrying when he was seven, in which case there was an eighteenth wife unaccounted for. How he ever moonlighted three times with that forty-year-old woman staggers the imagination.

Before a hungry mob of feminists, sexologists, and other mullahs descends on the case to extrapolate earth-shaking judgments, I herewith wish to stake a claim to the dramatic rights. In this tortuous, steamy maze of conflicting passions, I believe, repose the seeds of a powerful drama—possibly one like Joseph Hergesheimer's *Java Head*, wherein the lovely Chinese bride of a New England mariner (played, I recall, in the silent movie version by the incomparable Jetta Goudal) is subjected to the bigotry and scorn of his puritan townsfolk. Or it could be something on the order of *Alice of Old Vincennes*, sentimental yet rollicking. I just mention these two extremes to show how widely I propose to cast my net and see what we can scoop up. So if everyone will kindly shove back his chair a bit, we can improvise a little stage and begin. It'll be hours before those hooligans get back from Plato's Retreat.

SCENE: *The conservatory of Mucho Dinero, the Newport mansion of Bonanza and Wolfram Frontispiece, socially prominent leaders of the colony and longtime possessors of old money. A profusion of smilax, exotic plants, bibelots, and objets de vertu. Through the open French doors behind them is glimpsed Cliff Walk, along which occasionally saunter the figures of Mrs. Potter Palmer, Berry Wall, Mrs. Lytle Hull, Laddie Sanford, Mrs. T. Markoe Robertson, and other members of the gratin—an illusion achieved by cardboard cutouts of the foregoing drawn along a groove in the stage floor. At rise, Wolfram Frontispiece, white-thatched and peppery, paces to and fro chewing an unlit Havana, his brow furrowed. After a moment, Farkrimter, the butler, appears on the threshold.*

FARKRIMTER: Oh, excuse me, sir. I didn't realize the consistory was occupied.

FRONTISPIECE: Consistory? This is a conservatory, man. Don't you know the difference?

FARKRIMTER: Not really.

FRONTISPIECE: Then you'd be a hell of a guy to arrange a meeting of cardinals. What is it?

FARKRIMTER: The chauffeur phoned from the airport, sir. He's bringing your daughter Wheatena and her fiancé from

Benares, but there wasn't room in the Cadillac. The rest are coming by bus.

FRONTISPIECE: The rest of whom? We're not expecting anyone else.

FARKRIMTER: The seventeen Indian ladies with Dass Ist Kein Kint, your daughter's intended.

FRONTISPIECE (*taken aback*): Suffering catfish, what kind of fumadiddles is that brat of mine mixed up in now? Bonanza —Bonanza! . . . Where the devil's my wife?

FARKRIMTER: She's down in the basement, laundering some thousand-dollar bills.

FRONTISPIECE: Well, go get her—don't stand there like a wooden Indian! (*As there is a wooden Indian standing there, a statue of Massasoit, Farkrimter awaits clarification, but finally obeys.*) Humph, a pretty kettle of fish. I knew no good would come of it when that willful, capricious minx went off to study in that ashram. And then, to agitate us further, came word that she'd fallen in love with some handkerchief head twice her age. However, best not to fly off the handle; the fellow must be a rajah at least, seeing as how he's brought his retinue with him.

BONANZA (*Bursting in distractedly*): Oh, Wolfram, what ever shall we do? Willful, capricious Wheatena has just skyed in from her ashram with a handkerchief head—

FRONTISPIECE: Yes, yes, the audience knows all that. Farkrimter and I planted it in the exposition.

BONANZA: Then why did I burst in here distractedly?

FRONTISPIECE: To cover a stage wait until the couple and their female cortege arrive at our porte cochère below. (*A hubbub of voices ascending*) And here they are now, by Jove. I've a premonition these voyagers from the subcontinent may have a surprise in store. (*His intuition is faultless. Dass Ist Kein Kint, a frail and wrinkled Bengali clad in a dhoti, totters in supported by Wheatena Frontispiece. His face is as deeply seamed as Ramses II's, and he weighs sixty-three pounds soaking wet. Behind them comes a swarm of gaily plumaged women of varying age and hue in saris. Note: These last, in order for the ensuing dialogue to be heard, should be deftly shunted offstage to the kitchen by Farkrimter.*)

WHEATENA: Well, hello, everyone! My, Mucho Dinero is certainly a sight for sore eyes after that grotty ashram. (*Archly*) However, I daresay you menfolk have a lot to hash over between you, so Mummy and I will creep away to my old nursery for some girl talk. (*They exit, arms around each other's waist.*)

FRONTISPIECE (*a pause as he debates whether to clap his prospective son-in-law on the back*): Hiya, old man. Nice to have you on board.

DASS IST (*cups ear*): How's that?

FRONTISPIECE: I said—welcome. On Bailey's Beach you will hear the mermaids singing each to each. Have a cigar.

DASS IST: No, thank you. I am at present munching on some betel nuts.

FRONTISPIECE: Oh, sure—feel free. (*Nudges brass cuspidor toward him*) Ah—how are things over there in the sugarcane?

DASS IST: So-so. As the Lord Krishna says, cow dung cannot be gathered where no cow has been.

FRONTISPIECE: Hmm. This is not a problem we have in Newport, Rhode Island. (*Abruptly*) Say, how do you manage to chew that fodder? You haven't got a tooth in your head.

DASS IST: No, I lost my choppers—let me think—soon after the fall of Port Arthur to the Japanese, in 1905.

FRONTISPIECE: Yes, I noticed you had a bit of mileage on you. Might I inquire when you were born?

DASS IST: In 1857, during the Sepoy Rebellion. I'll be a hundred and twenty-two next July, he-he-he.

FRONTISPIECE: What are you giggling about?

DASS IST: Oh, the idea of me and Wheatena and all my ex-wives living in a spread like this. Boy, the Emperor Aurangzeb never had it so good.

FRONTISPIECE (*voice rising*): Ex-wives? See here, Clyde, are you concealing something from me?

DASS IST: Of course not. You saw them just now—the seventeen ladies that rode in on the bus. Also, I've been mousing around with a pharmacist in Jaipur, a lulu—

FRONTISPIECE: But I thought . . . (*Roaring*) Young man, you have the impudence to come in here seeking my daughter's hand—

DASS IST: Now, slow down, Pops, you're liable to blow a fuse. You want to wind up with blue lips and a tag on your feet?

FRONTISPIECE: Don't try to sweet-talk me, you insolent puppy! (*Rips open a bureau drawer; extracts a checkbook*) I know your sort. How much?

DASS IST (*dangerously*): Let's get this straight. Are you under the impression you can buy me off—that a scrap of paper could compensate me for the love of a creature as delicate as a startled fawn?

FRONTISPIECE: Money talks. Every man has his price.

DASS IST: In that case, we're in business. Speak up, fat man—how much is the white bird worth to you?

FRONTISPIECE (*his chuckle oilier than Sydney Greenstreet's*): By gad, sir, you *are* a caution. I like a man I can see through. By gad, sir, I like a man who can see through me. Why don't we meet somewhere, like Locke-Ober's, in Boston, and talk this thing over?

DASS IST: All right, but tell that gunsel of yours, Farkrimter, to keep his hands off me or I'll kill him. Also, we're going to need a fall guy—to pay for the lunch.

FRONTISPIECE: I'll bring along Farkrimter. The money he gets in kickbacks from my tradesmen, he could support I and you the rest of our days. And now, shall we join the nineteen ladies?

DASS IST: Frontispiece, I like your style. By gad, sir, you're a man after my own heart—but too many are after it, and the hormones are different. (*As they exit arm in arm*) Listen, how about you and your wife and what's-her-name coming over to the ashram next summer?

CURTAIN

Wanted: Short or Long Respite by Former Cinéaste

I often ask myself these days as I shell out four dollars, stumble over people's feet in the murk, and gingerly settle down on the slag of their popcorn just what sort of will-o'-the-wisp I'm still pursuing. Surely anyone marinated by sixty-five years' exposure to the silver screen, mile upon mile of acetate etched with the hallucinations of ribbon clerks and debauched waitresses, would be much better off at home sipping hot cocoa and reading Pascal's *Pensées* in his nightgown—they now have nightgowns embroidered with Pascal's thoughts—yet there I sit, slack-jawed, a grizzled prospector still avid for whatever nuggets might turn up in the sludge. To be candid, the only ones I hope to unearth someday were encapsulated, say my informants, in two foreign films of such unrelieved tedium that projectionists fainted away in their booths. The first was an Italian production, laid in ancient Greece, which bumbled along inexorably up to the moment its hero declined an invitation to dinner. "I really would love to come," he assured the host, "but we're having a dialogue at Plato's tonight." The second, a Mitteleuropean strudel based on the life of Mozart, contained a passage wherein the young genius trembling approached his patron, a Herr Mossbach, for an estimate of his latest work. The verdict, alas, was devastating, and Mozart, streaked with tears, tottered out into the snow. Waiting on the corner, his confidant, Bill Eugenspiel, refused to be daunted by the news. "Courage, Wolfgang," he said, clapping him cheerily on the back. "Who cares what that old mossback thinks? Let us go and compose *The Magic Flute.*"

While treasures as dazzling as these are of a rarity beyond price, it should be noted that there are equally precious ones that were never recorded on film but that sparkle in the memory of graybeards like yours truly, who was once connected with the cinema. During the spring of 1935, I was briefly employed at Warner Brothers–First National studio in Burbank, spot-welding the dialogue on a number of its pictures. Among the dozen or so screenwriters on the assembly line, which included Flotsman and Jetsman, a team that wrote several gangster classics, was one Winston Finston, a scholarly, withdrawn chap with a hearing aid, whose deafness, mercifully, shielded him from our boisterous witticisms. His particular achievement, I learned, was that he had furnished the idea for *Dr. Ehrlich's Magic Bullet*, the movie, starring Edward G. Robinson, about the epochal discovery of arsphenamine, the anti-syphilitic compound marketed as Salvarsan. Even had Finston and I been marooned together on a desert island, however, the pallid spirochete would have been a dubious basis for friendship, and in due course we left the lot without exchanging so much as an imprecation about its godhead, Darryl Zanuck.

A decade passed before I heard of the man again, and then in a context so different that it defied credulity. Shortly after Pearl Harbor, Finston, despite other seeming disabilities, like flat feet and membership in the Consumers Union, had applied for entry into the United States Marine Corps and been accepted. His experience gained as a screenwriter enabled him to survive the rigorous training of the Corps. He scrambled through mire, demonstrated he could eviscerate any opponent, and in general displayed sufficient barbarity under pressure to qualify him for jungle warfare. Shortly thereafter, his outfit received a forty-eight-hour leave, along with the strict admonition to hold itself ready to be shipped out. Four days later, a couple of burly M.P.s ransacking the Los Angeles area for strays came abreast of a renowned delicatessen called Woloshin's, on La Brea just off Wilshire. Through the window they caught sight of a figure in Marine uniform staging a culinary orgy. A cornucopia of smoked salmon, sturgeon, pastrami, corned beef, chopped liver, sauerkraut, dill pickles, sour tomatoes, rye bread, bagels, and seeded rolls ranged before him, Finston sat, chewing blissfully, his eyes closed and hearing aid switched off—a man literally at ease in Zion. His bubble, woefully, burst in a twinkling when the M.P.s yanked him to his feet and branded him AWOL.

"I'm not! I'm not!" he pleaded. "They sent me here!"

His captors gaped at him. "They what?"

"They told me to go to Woloshin's."

"Not Woloshin's, you fool," they cried in outrage. "The *Aleutians!*"

Came postwar Hollywood, when McCarthy's tumbrels rolled and the mournful cry of the fink—"Bring out your dead heresies"—resounded through the streets. From Azusa to the shores of Malibu, from the throne of Harry Cohn, at Columbia, to the cardboard spires of M-G-M, where Louis B. Mayer and Dore Schary were suzerain, dissent was hushed, and no man gave ear to his neighbor lest Communist henbane be poured in while he nodded. Under the iron heel, the crucible well-nigh cracked, but along with the dross it produced one gem of purest ray serene. Its mineral elements, so to speak, were two—Keenan Wynn, the actor, and an executive at M-G-M named Serge Kolodny. The latter, a porcine type akin to those that root out truffles in Périgord, had been chosen by management to sniff out lurking subversives, and though Wynn bore no taint, he had been observed at meetings of the Hollywood Anti-Nazi League, a supposed branch of the Comintern. Inviting the young man to his office, Kolodny proceeded to massage his ego with chicken fat. Like his immortal sire, greatest of all comedians, Keenan was B.O. dynamite, the most blazing talent since Warren William, and Clark Gable's own choice to inherit his mantle.

Hence it was imperative to inoculate him against insidious foreign doctrines. Could Keenan by any chance, he asked silkily, recall the names of any individuals he had encountered at the Hollywood Anti-Nazi League?

"Jiminy crickets," Wynn protested. "I meet hundreds of people every day, Mr. Kolodny. I never listen to their names, I just autograph—"

"Of course, my boy," his inquisitor soothed him. "Nobody could answer a question like that off the top of their head. Now, why don't you go home, have a couple of highballs and a good feed, and tomorrow, when your brain clears, we'll have another chat—O.K.? . . . By the way," he called out as Wynn was closing the door, "the option of your contract's just coming up for renewal, isn't it?"

A sudden, inexplicable fantasy that he was being drawn up into Kolodny's snout as into a vacuum cleaner seized the actor, and he left hurriedly.

The interrogation resumed next day, with Kolodny using every means short of threat to elicit the identity of the League's conspirators. In vain, he wheedled, flattered, cooed. Wynn's forehead beaded over with perspiration as he lashed his memory to no purpose. All he could recollect, he asserted, was a sea of faces, speeches, applause.

The other man resorted to guile. "The human mind is like a maze," he pronounced, formulating what might be termed Kolodny's Law. "The more you hock away on it, the less you can drain out. Now," he added, with apparent irrelevance, "I understand you're very fond of motorcycling. Is that correct?"

Wynn signified it was.

"Then forget everything we said. Take a carefree little spin on your wheel—go to Vegas, Tijuana, lay in the sun and commute with nature. Remember what Shakespeare said: 'Where the bee sucks, there suck I.' By Monday, you'll be as fresh as a baby, ready to spill out names, dates, all that poison they fed you."

Three days thence, Wynn sat once more in Kolodny's office, oil-stained and travel-worn, fiddling with the helmet and goggles in his lap. "The next night, we went on to Bakersfield," he re-counted. "After dinner, I shot some pool there—"

"Yes, yes, must have been a great trip," Kolodny said impatiently. "You look fabulous, Kennan. But, getting back to our little problem—did you at least think of one person you recognized at those League meetings?"

As Wynn hesitated and nodded slowly, Kolodny half rose from his chair. "Who, who?" he fluted like a barn owl.

"Dore Schary," said the actor.

Kolodny's face went livid. "What the hell, kid, you're only human," he sputtered. "If you can't remember, you . . . can't . . . *remember!*"

Among the regrets most of us harbor in common, I daresay, is the wish that we could have been a fly on the wall at some colloquy of the great. I once grew dizzy when Sax Rohmer, the creator of Dr. Fu Manchu, in the course of narrating some trifling incident observed, "At the time, I was strolling arm in arm with E. Phillips Oppenheim at a hotel in Evian-les-Bains." Similarly, what a privilege it would have been to eavesdrop on Dashiell Hammett and Raymond Chandler at the dinner *Black Mask* gave its contributors in the twenties, even though each swore he was unconscious of the other's presence. No less historic was an occasion in 1933 when two celebrated poets converged in Hollywood, giving rise to a line that lit up the sky like Vesuvius. Flies on the wall there were none, but one of the duo, e. e. cummings, generously confided the details many years later.

"God knows what I was doing on the Coast," he said. "Some impresario with a pointy head had read my play *him* and thought it would make a good musical for Jeanette MacDonald and Bertrand Russell, so Marian and I went out to see if there was any catch. There was—he wanted me to play Russell, in a sailor suit. Well, when that fell through, we figured what the dickens, you're only dead once, let's be real Angelenos. So we

visited the homes of the stars, watched the grunion run at Santa
Monica, drank malted milks too thick for a straw—it was
stupendous. Those people really know how to get the marrow
out of life." He paused, obviously derailed by a random memory.
"Say, who was the fat poet who used to hang around Lee
Chumley's place down here in the old days?"

"Fat poet?" I pondered. "Would it be Eli Siegel, who wrote
'Hot Afternoons Have Been in Montana'? He was thin, but his
poetry was quite fat."

"No, no, this one wrote light verse. Used to contribute to
F.P.A.'s 'Conning Tower' in the *World*. . . . Well, doesn't
matter. Anyway, just before we left L.A., some face card in the
movie colony invited us to a party, a very stylish affair, in a
gorge called Pussy Willow Canyon—or am I making that up?"

I assured him that naught was impossible in the Land of Nod.

"Well, we had a devil of a time finding the place—drove up
and down endless ravines, blundered into the wrong haciendas,
châteaus, palazzos—and finally got there an hour late. The house
was lit up like Versailles. Rivers of champagne, two hundred
magnificoes milling around the lawns—it was a floorwalker's
idea of heaven." He stopped again. "Look, this fat poet whose
name escapes me—you must remember him. He was pretty well
known; in fact, he wrote some very sprightly stuff for the old
Life and *Vanity Fair*."

"I can't think who you mean. Wait a second—could it have
been Louis Untermeyer or Arthur Guiterman?"

He brightened. "Yes, the same *galère*, the W. S. Gilbert school,
but it wasn't either of them. Oh, well, it'll come to me. So there
we were at this shindig, Maid Marian and I, strutting around
with the other peacocks. Eftsoon, some rake like Lew Cody or
Lowell Sherman besought her to trip the light fantastic, and
away they whirled to the strains of 'There's Danger in Your
Eyes, Chérie.' Just as I was heading for the bar, someone grabbed
my shoulder, spun me around, and wrapped me in an embrace,
drenching my shirtfront with his tears. It was this poet from
Chumley's. He'd been out there writing movies for fifteen
years— And now I remember his name. 'Look on me, *cher*

maître, and have pity,' he was sobbing. 'You knew me when I was Sam Hoffenstein, a bard. Cummings, I'm a whore!' "

But, of course, that was just a metaphor. I worked in the place. They never made any of us wear kimonos.

Portrait of the Artist
as a Young Cat's-Paw

The other evening, I was rummaging around in my bureau for a Belmont-style celluloid collar, slightly yellowed by age, that I planned to wear with my pongee suit and a lawn tie when the weather got warmer. This was the same outfit in which I posed for J. C. Leyendecker in those ads he drew for Kuppenheimer and for Hart Schaffner & Marx; you probably remember me also as his Arrow-collar model. Anyhow, during my search I pulled the bureau away from the wall and found a book I'd repeatedly flung there in exasperation while reading it. Its title was *James Joyce: A Portrait of the Artist*, by Stan Gébler Davies, and wild horses—nay, Percherons, Clydesdales, and Suffolk punches yoked together—will not persuade me to confess my lack of admiration for its author. Mr. Davies, a Dubliner, is identified in a biographical note as born in 1943 and "an enthusiastic Joycean since his discovery at the age of thirteen of an illicit copy of *Ulysses*." (It was illicit in Ireland at the time.) Nowhere in his book, sad to say, does he describe his euphoria on that occasion, so we can only imagine him cracking his knuckles and exclaiming "Hot spit!" as he floated down Molly Bloom's stream of consciousness in the final chapter.

Curiously enough, it was this very topic, the once illicit status of *Ulysses* in the United States, that prompted Davies to write the one passage arresting enough to make me cease—if only temporarily—flinging the book against the wall. It read, "Forty copies were smuggled across the Ontario border by Barnet Braverman, a friend of Hemingway's (the Canadians had unaccountably failed to ban *Ulysses*). Mr. Braverman crossed by ferry from Windsor to Detroit once a day with two copies making an alarming bulge front and rear of him, eyed suspiciously by U.S. Customs. But they, as it happened, were more eager in those days to suppress booze than literature."

Mr. Braverman's contraband echoes in memory the account my wife gave me of returning from her maiden voyage to Europe, also during Prohibition. She was accompanied by her mother, who in turn was accompanied by sixteen minute bottles of liqueur— Bénédictine, Chartreuse, anisette, and the like. To get past the lynx-eyed customs inspectors, they were suspended from her mother's girdle in a fringe of sixteen little hammocks the elder had crocheted aboard ship. Apart from tinkling like the Swiss bell ringers then favored in vaudeville, the bottles reached home undetected, as did the copy of *Ulysses* secreted in some silken recess of the ladies' steamer trunk.

I myself bore home a copy of the sacred text from my initial trip overseas, but I also brought back a package that caused me far more inquietude. To put the story into perspective and a nutshell, I undertook the trip because two other marine excursions had bombed. In the spring of 1927, I occupied a wee studio on West Ninth Street in the Village, where I drew cartoons that ultimately lowered the circulation of a weekly named *Judge* to the vanishing point. The studio had a north skylight and the approved décor of the period—primrose-yellow walls, a Roman daybed with slipcover of monk's cloth, and a lamp consisting of a huge glass carboy and a parchment shade that excluded all light. It was on the sixth floor of a building equidistant from the Athens Chop House and a restaurant run by the Siegel brothers, and, what with my meagre sustenance and my constant toiling up those five flights, I became so thin that a Siegel brother inadvertently stuck me in a jardiniere, mistaking me for an umbrella. Realizing that my dream of bankrupting *Judge* was futile unless I recovered my strength,

I went around asking people did they know a place a man could get away for a while.

They vouchsafed that they did indeed. They hadn't been there themselves, but everyone said that Martha's Vineyard was the Garden of Eden, only less crowded. That was what I was looking for—a roomy spot where one didn't have to stand in jardinieres. So I packed up all my gear, the bristol board, the Higgins India Ink, the Chinese white, and the fixative, and, bent double like a Sherpa, caught a train to New Bedford and a steamer down to Vineyard Sound. Well, one look at the salt-water taffy and that merry-go-round in Oak Bluffs—the Flying Horses—and the gingerbread houses in Cottage City, and I pelted back to the vessel. Eighteen years were to pass before I discovered what I'd missed.

My second journey offshore, to Fire Island, was a similar epiphany. Somewhere between the ferry landing and the Ocean Beach Inn, a distance of thirty feet, I contracted a virulent case of poison ivy. For the next six days, snow-white with calamine lotion and more heavily bandaged than Claude Rains in *The Invisible Man*, I sat in a second-floor room of the inn, inhaling the scent of fried clams drifting up the stairway. Desperate for contact with anyone, even the management, I offered to type their menus for free, but they refused, fearing that my touch would infect the bill of fare. Incensed, I determined to emulate Bet-a-Million Gates—to purchase the hotel and fire the whole bloody lot of them. The impulse waned, and the moment my affliction did I took leave of the sandspit pronto.

It was, hence, without any appetite whatever for travel that on returning to New York I strayed by chance into a UFA film called *Variety*. In it Emil Jannings, Lya de Putti, and Warwick Ward composed a troupe of aerialists whose career ends in mayhem when Miss de Putti switches her affections from Jannings to Ward. The key scenes took place in Berlin's renowned cabaret the Wintergarten. Why the picture evoked in me a burning desire to visit the Wintergarten, and, moreover, how I dug up the wherewithal, I cannot fathom, but one month thereafter the S.S. *Leviathan* was bound east for Cherbourg and

I was on her second-class manifest. So were Francesca Wild and
Bunny Huggins.

Francesca and Bunny, two lovelies newly hatched from some
incubator like Mount Holyoke or Wheaton, were well calcu-
lated to ravish the Old World or anyone on his way to it. A
frail, blond Angelica Kauffmann type of beauty, Francesca was
clad in what seemed to be moonbeams, but I could be wrong
about that. Bunny was dark and vivid—lots of eyeshadow and
lipstick—with a divine figure, the kind that makes men yearn to
wrap its possessor in twenty-thousand-dollar sable coats. (I could
not only be wrong about that—I could be talking through my
hat.) The voyage had scarcely begun when a turn of fate threw
us together. I was quietly sketching away in the bar, unaware
that the two were at the adjoining table. Suddenly Bunny leaned
over and inquired if I was an artist.

"The reason I ask," she explained, "is that you can't fail to
have noticed that I'm wearing a black tailored suit and blouse
set off by a bunch of foamy white lace at the chest. My friend
and I are at loggerheads anent the correct term for this frizzy
accessory. You being an artist, would not ephemera of this sort
fall naturally within your purview?"

"Why, yes," I said. "I believe it can be variously described as
a jabot or as a fichu or as ruching. Under whatever designation,
Mademoiselle," I said, rising and kissing her hand, "it has never
been more enchantingly displayed."

"*Tiens*, Francesca," she exclaimed, coloring to the roots of
her hair, "I declare, we must have bunked into Monsieur
Beaucaire himself! Shall we invite Mr. Valentino to join us?"

From that point on, the three of us were inseparable, the
balance of the trip a kaleidoscope of shuffleboard, quaffing
bouillon, with saltines, in our deck chairs, wearing paper hats
at the captain's gala, and little other activity, since smooching
in lifeboats was alien to our moral code, and, besides, impossible
when you are three people. In due course, we steamed into
Queenstown and were welcomed with a cornet solo of "When
Irish Eyes Are Smiling," performed by an alcoholist teetering
uncertainly in a dory. At Southampton, amid emotional fare-

wells, the girls debarked and I proceeded onward to the Continent.

The pilgrimage to Berlin's Wintergarten took its place reasonably high on the list of debacles in my experience. There were, of course, no aerialists executing triple somersaults around the rafters of the cabaret. Instead, two dozen Central Europeans sought valiantly with throats, feet, accordions, Indian clubs, playing cards, and magic equipment to demonstrate their crippling lack of talent. Meanwhile, I sat by drinking sweet Tokay that turned to crystals of sugar on my lips. But ultimately there came deliverance. In an American jazz group that headlined the show I recognized a former classmate, and to him I dispatched an SOS. The good man did his best, according to his lights. He and several fellow-bandsmen conducted me on a tour of various bars in the Kurfürstendamm district, where they painstakingly collected the ingredients of a monumental hangover and presented it to me at the railway station. As the milk train crawled back to Paris, every piston stroke of the engine athrob in my brain, I became in fancy that detestable stereotype who has imbibed too freely, the wealthy young rounder cowering under an ice bag applied by his devoted manservant. Such was my relief when the delirium ceased that on arriving at the Gare du Nord I knelt down and promised the stationmaster I would never touch another drop of sweet Tokay—a pledge I have kept to this day.

In the week following, I alternated from the Dôme to the Select to the Rotonde to the Closerie-des-Lilas, eavesdropping on folk I thought might be the originals of Jake Barnes, Lady Brett, and Bill Gorton, and when I found they were eavesdropping on me under the same misapprehension, I decided we were all a lost generation and booked a trip homeward on the *Berengaria*. A couple of days before sailing, I ran into Francesca and Bunny having a pressed citron at the Two

Maggots. With them was an elderly woman, a Mrs. Wolf or Fox, or some such predator. We had a nice reunion, and possibly I took one more thimble of Dubonnet than I usually elect to have.

"So this is your first trip to Paris, Mr. Praline," says this Fox person cunningly. "I suppose you've bought a lot of gifts over here for your girlfriends back in New York, tee-hee."

No, blurts out the wealthy young rounder and authority on the high trapeze, only around sixty dollars' worth. It's a wonder I didn't hand her my watch and chain and billfold, too, while I was at it.

"Oh, you don't say." If I'd looked at her instead of snapping my suspenders, I could have seen her salivating. "I wonder, Fran and Bun, whether your handsome, courteous young friend could do me a teensy-weensy favor."

"What is it, what is it?" they clamored, adding in feminine sign language, "Honey, after that last drink, this mark is putty in your hands."

Well Mr. Protheroe it's too sweet my son's about to be married in New York and I bought him a bed at the Galeries Lafayette or Le Printemps I forget which but I have the receipt right here in my bag there look at it just forty dollars now to ship it would take months and months but since you're going over it won't be a bit of trouble to declare it just hand them this receipt I'll arrange everything with the store the bed'll be loaded on the ship Stanley will be waiting on the pier God bless you Mr. Proskauer for understanding a mother's heart full to overflowing with gratitude.

The old harpy never could have euchred me into it but for those two precious shipmates of mine wheedling and needling me to help her, and, who knows, they may have slipped something into my drink. At any rate, a week later the assistant purser on the *Berengaria* notified me they had a case in the hold, bearing my name. He thought it might be quite sizable, because the Cunarder's bow had been awash ever since we sailed. He thought there might be a bit of a delay unloading it on arrival, as the three winches were kept pretty busy.

"Not half so busy as the three winches—wenches—were kept who were loading it," I growled. I had to repeat it several times before he got it.

His sombre prediction was realized in spades. The *Berengaria*'s fires werc long since banked, my fellow-passengers had departed hours earlier, and still I sat in the customs shed, grinding my teeth and composing sulphurous limericks about Mrs. Fox. Finally, two inspectors materialized and signalled me to follow. In an area heaped with boxes and bales lay a wooden case large enough to accommodate an A.C.F. cruiser. The inspectors examined my customs declaration, her receipt, and the bill of lading the purser had given me.

"Here, hand me that pinch bar," said one. "I want a look at the contents of this box."

The *contents*—that was the word that demolished my house of cards. Who knew what was inside there? It could be opium, the Romanov jewels, half a dozen illegal Chinese. Oh, what a blithering idiot I had been! Wait, Officer, I wish to make a full-breasted disclosure—I mean I want to turn state's evidence. It's too late; he's torn away the board. Thank heaven—a mattress! Still, there could be dope inside. . . .

"Look, you claim you paid forty dollars for this bed," said the other inspector. "Are you aware they retail wholesale for a hundred and eighty?"

"I—I don't understand," I said, and tried to entrap him in semantics. "If it's retail, how can it be wholesale, too?"

"Oh, a wisenheimer, eh?" His voice rose an octave. "Let me see your passport, you."

"Hold it, Vic. Le me handle this," his colleague interposed. "Listen, bub, what are you—a dealer, an importer? Or is this article for your own use? No monkeyshines, now—remember, you're under oath."

With visions of myself striped like a zebra and stitching mailbags, I realized there was only one recourse: I would have to stoop to the level of Mrs. Fox. I assumed what I hoped was a syrupy, lovesick expression. "Well, gentlemen, to tell you the truth, I'm engaged to the dearest, sweetest girl in the whole wide world, and we're to be married next week." I paused and pulled out the vox-humana stop. "I brought this over for our little nest."

Averted though were my eyes in shame and self-loathing, I could tell nevertheless that I had struck pay dirt. I heard their commingled sighs of *Brüderschaft*.

"Well, that's different. . . . Sure, whyn't you say so before? . . . Good luck, my boy. . . . Here's your receipt. Run along, fella."

When I reached the barrier, it took no genius to distinguish the legitimate bridegroom-to-be. Tentacles outstretched, he was preparing to smother me with gratitude, buy me seven-course meals at Villepigue's in Sheepshead Bay, treat me to countless weekends at Grossinger's, but I threw him the receipt and split. Up those vertiginous stairs I went to my studio, and before long I was cartooning away as good as new. It was hardly an ideal occupation, but it was a damn sight easier than smuggling.

One Order of Blintzes,
and Hold the Flimflam

A light rain was falling on the just and the unjust alike, and my cheeks glowed like twin pippins that February evening when I flung open the door of Cooper's Dairy Restaurant, on the lower East Side, and paused for breath. If my rosy flush suggested anticipation for the cuisine within, it was illusory; the operatic entrance and heaving bosom arose from overexertion. Dining at Cooper's demands a sprint along one of the most sinister crosstown blocks in New York—so fearsome, in fact, that it was chosen for a bloodcurling sequence in the film *Taxi Driver*, and he who would arrive with wallet and skin intact must be as fleet as the chamois. Except for the horns, knock wood, I was that chamois.

My quick survey of the interior was reassuring. A few somnolent patrons lingered at the Formica-topped tables, and, selecting the remotest—of the tables, that is; only a Rorschach could have evaluated the patrons—I spread my paperback against a hillock of seed rolls and prepared to consume my meal in peace. Everything boded well; the waiter's face wore its customary expression of gloomy martyrdom, the borscht had slopped over the bowl as tradition requires, and I settled down to the anthology of Simenon in the certitude that nothing on earth aids digestion like a velvety mixture of beets, sour cream, and murder.

Ten minutes into the mélange, the first streaks of dawn had silvered the windows of the Police Judiciaire on the Quai des Orfèvres, Maigret's brow was furrowed into corduroy over the strangulation of a prostitute in the Rue de Lappe, and naught but a telltale red smear remained where once was borscht. Then a deep, rather peremptory voice jerked me back into the present.

"Mind if I sit here, friend? They've closed the other section."

Had Maigret himself suddenly appeared in Cooper's and busted me for garrotting the *nymphe du pavé*, it would have surprised me less than the speaker. His corpulent figure was encased in a mink-collared overcoat set off by a midnight-blue homburg, and as he negligently drew off gray gloves and rested his malacca stick and alligator attaché case on a chair, I found my tongue with an effort.

"Er—no, of course not. I'm just boning up for my exam."

"Oh?" A hint of condescension tinged his paternal smile. "You're a student, are you?"

Too grizzled to masquerade as a rookie at the Police Academy, I opted for a safer identity. "Extension course at the New School," I said briefly, plucking a salt stengel from the bread basket. "Detective Fiction Since Edgar Allan Poe."

"Interesting," he commented. His smile broadened. "I suppose it's taught you a whole lot about the criminal mind?"

"I know plenty already," I said. "The business I'm in, Mac, you have to be a pretty shrewd judge of human nature."

"And what is that?" he asked, twinkling down from Parnassus.

"Yard goods," I said. "You know, mill ends and remnants— me and my brother run a store on Fourteenth Street. Boy, do we skin those Porto Ricans!"

It could have been my imagination, but from where I sat I heard a muffled click. In a flash, the grand-seigneurial manner switched to a wet shine in the eyes which was pure larceny. As he leaned forward intently, he came into focus—J. Rufus Wallingford, urging me to become expansive.

"I guess you two do all right there."

"You can say that again." I hooked thumbs into armpits. "Got a split-level rancher in Great Neck that cost three-fifty big ones, a Caddy Seville, and a paid-up annuity worth four hundred grand. I could quit tomorrow, except I still enjoy raking it in."

Our waiter, arms akimbo and stony-faced, had forborne to interrupt, but now his impatience, like the borscht, bubbled over. "Please, we're not running here a retirement village. Did you decide?"

"Ah, yes, yes, I must order." My tablemate caught up the menu and scanned it with obvious incomprehension. "Protose steak . . . eggplant cutlets . . . I don't recognize any of these dishes. Is this some kind of ethnic place?"

"Well, sort of—they get a good many Albanians. Bring me an order of cheese blintzes and a glass of tea."

"Cheese blintzes?" the stranger repeated doubtfully. "What are they?"

"Crêpes, dumplings. Little sachets of heartburn which lay on the stomach like lead. They come with blueberries and cherries if you prefer."

"Fine, fine. I'll have the same." His computer, plainly, was still calculating my net worth, which must have come up trumps, for he launched straightaway into the capework. "Sorry, I should have introduced myself. J. Willis Wainwright, vice-president of the Gripfast Mucilage Company, in Ashtabula."

"Jud Kluckhorn," I responded.

"A pleasure to meet you, sir. Say, I knew a Kluckhorn once— a fry cook at a lumber camp in Manitoba. Fritz Kluckhorn, a great fellow."

"No relation, but all us Kluckhorns are kooks. Ah-ha-ha."

"Ah-ha-ha. But to turn serious for a moment. You know, we do a lot of business in England, so I often see their newspapers. Are you familiar with the London *Times*? . . . Too bad. They run some marvellous crime stories—just the kind you're studying. However, that's beside the point." He withdrew a folded clipping. "Have a peek at this article they printed the other day."

Headlined "SAUDI PAYS £8.8M FOR WILDENSTEIN COLLEC-
TION," the account read:

The Wildenstein family collection of French furniture and works
of art, considered by the art world more distinguished than that of
Mentmore, has been acquired by a Saudi Arabian businessman, Mr.
Akram Ojjeh, for 75m francs (£8.8m). Last week it was announced
that he had bought The France, the transatlantic liner, for 80m
francs. He now plans to combine his two purchases, exhibiting the
202 superb Wildenstein items on board The France, according to
the Lebanese weekly, As Sayad. The liner will be anchored off the
coast of Florida and probably run as an hotel. According to Reuter
and Agence France-Presse, Mr. Ojjeh was born in Syria and became
a naturalized Saudi citizen in 1950. His fortune appears to be based
on his company, Technique d'Avant Garde Finance, hitherto noted
for high quality prefabricated buildings. The company has had
several very large contracts in Saudi Arabia and is believed to have
connexions with the Royal Family.

"Like, wow, man," I said, wide-eyed. "That's going to be
some hotel. Maybe I'll take Bernice and the kids there someday
instead of the Fountainblue."

"Yes siree, and you'll be able to afford it!" Wainwright declared. "Why do I say that? I'll tell you why I say that. Because
you're going to be one of the owners!"

I stared at him, incredulous. "I am?"

"Sure—right up there with the biggies." He cast a hurried
glance about. "Better lower our voices—that waiter's snooping
around. I can't go into the fine points right now, but here's the
action. Through a source I'm not at liberty to disclose, I've
learned that this Saudi, this Akram Ojjeh, is under-financed.
He's in a sticky position—the banks are holding a lot of his
paper."

"You don't say. Did they tell you?"

"Nobody has to. I'm in the mucilage business, man. Paper,
mucilage, accountancy—it's all related."

"You mean one accountant tells another," I murmured
craftily.

"I knew I couldn't keep anything from a sly fox like you. Now, you're a smart businessman, Kluckhorn. Given his situation, what would you do?"

I pondered. "Well, I'd take back the paper and print on it 'Fire Sale' in big letters. Then I'd hang up a bunch of schmottas outside our store on Fourteenth Street."

"God almighty, what's eating you?" Wainwright snapped. "This is a deal involving millions, not like that flytrap of yours." He quailed as my face darkened. "Er—excuse me, no disrespect intended. What I'm getting at is, several associates and I have formed a little syndicate to help Mr. Ojjeh out of his difficulties. Each of us is contributing a hundred and seventy-five thousand dollars to the pot, in return for which we receive fifty-one per cent of the hotel stock. You follow?"

"Yes, but talk slower, I'm afraid I'll miss something. Do you think— I mean, if an outsider—" I swallowed and plunged ahead. "Is there room for just one more investor in the syndicate?"

"Well, I'd have to consult my partners in the consortium, naturally, but I think we might be able to squeeze you in. Time, however, is of the essence, so if I could have a small check as evidence of your good faith . . ."

About how much, did you figure?"

He sponged the trickle of saliva from his necktie. "Oh, the amount is academic—we'd put it in escrow until the formal agreement's signed. Say about half—ninety thousand dollars."

"Hmm, that's not chopped liver— Oops, did you hear that? I mentioned chopped liver in a dairy restaurant!"

"I heard it," he said shortly. "Well, what's the answer? Are you coming in? I have to cable Lausanne."

"Wait, don't rush me. . . . Ninety thousand dollars. . . . No, I'd like to talk it over with my brother first."

"Is that all?" His sudden gaiety was almost infectious. "Why don't we pop over and see him together?"

"Oh, we can't do that." I drew back. "He's in intensive care at Beth Israel Hospital. He was freezing a bunion on his foot with dry ice. It burned a hole in the floor and he fell into the cellar."

Wainwright stared at me fixedly for a moment. "Would you mind just repeating that?"

"No, I couldn't bear to," I said decisively. "It's too painful. But I'll tell you what. You've been so generous that I'm going to squeeze *you* in on something. From time to time, I experience what are called reading reversals, and I had one a moment ago when you showed me that clipping."

"Look here, Kluckhorn," he began, inflating himself like a blowfish. "I fail to see what connection—"

"It'll dawn on you presently," I assured him. "Pray, examine the name of this Saudi gentleman you're befriending—Akram Ojjeh. If you reverse it, as I did, you will get 'hejjo marka.' Substituting two letters and eliding one, it becomes 'hello mark,' and since 'mark' is the usual synonym in your calling for a chump or a pigeon, we obtain the answer to your proposal. Do you remember Texas Guinan's renowned salutation to customers at her night club, 'Hello, sucker!'?"

His face slowly turned ruddier—a phenomenon almost impossible to credit. "Are you by any chance—" he sputtered, and then checked himself. "Are you alleging that my associates and I are a pack of swindlers?"

"Hardly," I replied. "To do so would usurp the function of a district attorney. Besides, I question the collective term 'pack' that you employ. While eminently proper for hounds or wolves, would it not be more accurate to describe yourselves as a goniff of swindlers?"

"Listen, wise guy," he burst forth threateningly. "Don't play games with me!"

"Wainwright, be reasonable," I chided him. "One minute you're courting me to join your caper, the next you flatly reject me. Vacillation like that can mean only one thing—our brief love affair is over. I must ask you to leave this table."

For years, despite the assurances of popular fiction, I always doubted whether overwrought individuals gave vent to their feelings with a frustrated "Bah!" and stormed out, but now it was confirmed. With a frustrated "Bah!," Wainwright snatched up his impedimenta and tore out of Cooper's like a shot off a shovel. Simultaneously, our waiter emerged from the kitchen juggling two plates and a glass of tea.

"Hoo ha!" he exclaimed, mystified. "Where's the other party? Did he lose his appetite?"

"No, his impetus, I'd say."

"Well, I'll look around under the tables," he promised. "Meantime, what about his blintzes? Could you eat them, too?"

I shook my head.

"Then maybe you'll take them with you?"

"O.K.," I agreed, "but don't wrap them. I'll need them as weapons on the run home."

That's the great thing about Cooper's. Between the food and the trip there and back, you may not survive. Still, you meet some very unusual people.

PART TWO

The Hindsight Saga
Fragments of an
Autobiography

The Marx Brothers
Nathanael West
Dorothy Parker
Three Little Photoplays
  and How They Grew

The Marx Brothers

One October evening in the fall of 1931, a few minutes after
the curtain had risen on the second act of *Animal Crackers*, a
musical comedy starring the Four Marx Brothers, the occupant
of the seat adjoining mine, a comely person with a mink coat
folded on her lap, suddenly reached through it and twitched
my sleeve. I was then, and still fatuously conceive myself to be,
a hot-blooded young man; and if I did not respond immediately,
there were several cogent reasons. To begin with, the occupant
of the *other* seat adjoining mine, whom I had espoused a couple
of years before, was holding hands with me, so that I had none
left over to twitch back. Furthermore, the custodian of the lady
in mink, I had observed during the entr'acte, was a chap with
an undershot jaw and a beefy neck, the kind of lout I knew
would tolerate no poaching. More important than either consideration, however, was the fact that I was breathlessly and
rapturously absorbed in Groucho's courtship onstage of the
immortal Margaret Dumont, impersonating a dowager named
Mrs. Rittenhouse. It was at least five seconds, accordingly, before
I realized that my neighbor was extending a note and gesticu-
lating toward an usher in the aisle to indicate its source. Strain-
ing to decipher the message in the half darkness, I grew almost
dizzy with exultation. Mr. Marx acknowledged the card I had
sent in during the break to express my admiration, and re-
quested me to call on him backstage after the show.

While our meeting was in no sense epochal, it did have an

unpredictable consequence, and my forehead, to say nothing of
my career, might have been far less wrinkled had I not paid this
fortuitous homage. For the half-dozen years preceding, I had
been a contributor, in the dual capacity of artist and writer, to
Judge and *College Humor*. Both these magazines, during my
undergraduate days at Brown University, had reprinted drawings I had done for the college periodical, and when faced with
the choice of a livelihood, I turned naturally (if naïvely) to
comic art. There were vicissitudes that seemed insurmountable
at the time, but thanks to a stomach that shrank as they arose, I
managed to weather them. About the end of 1928, my work was
appearing in some profusion, and Horace Liveright, whose
daring as a publisher verged on audacity, brought out a collection of it called *Dawn Ginsbergh's Revenge*. It was a curious
little volume, bound in the horripilating green plush called
"flock" used to upholster railroad chairs, and as far as one could
tell, it had only two distinctive aspects. The title page omitted
any mention whatever of an author—I presumably was so over-
awed at the permanence I was achieving that I neglected to
check this detail—and the dust jacket bore a blurb from,
coincidentally, Groucho Marx. It read: "From the moment I
picked up your book until I laid it down, I was convulsed with
laughter. Some day I intend reading it."

To say, therefore, that I had set the Thames on fire by that
fateful evening in 1931 would be hardly accurate. The brush
and quill were yielding a pittance which I had persuaded the
idealistic lady whose hand I held to share with me, and through
some legerdemain we had managed to squeeze in two summers
abroad on the cheap. But the magazines I worked for were
feeling the Depression, and all of a sudden the barometer began
to fall. I started receiving a trickle of letters from the bank that
soon grew into a cascade. Perhaps, its officials hinted delicately,
I would like to transfer to some bank that had facilities for
handling smaller accounts. Maybe I didn't need a bank after all,
they hazarded, but merely a mattress or a loose brick in the fireplace. A deep cleft, resembling the Rift Valley in East Africa,
appeared between my eyebrows about the first of every month.

Beyond rending my clothes or dropping an occasional reference to the poorhouse, though, I was careful to conceal my anxieties from my helpmate. Whether she suspected anything from the newspaper recipes I left around the kitchen, cheap but hearty agglomerations of macaroni and tuna fish, I cannot say. If she did, she gave no hint of it.

This was our approximate situation, then, at the moment the summons from Groucho arrived, and it was without any portent that the encounter would be fateful that I hastened backstage after the performance. Once, however, we had exchanged cordialities—a bit awkward for my wife since Groucho was clad only in his shorts—he breezily confessed to an ulterior purpose in his invitation. One of the networks had latterly been entreating the Marxes to appear in a radio series, and he wondered if I could be cozened into writing it. Flattering as I found his esteem, I was frankly overwhelmed.

"I—I wouldn't know how to begin," I faltered. "I've never worked on a radio script."

"Neither has Will Johnstone," admitted Groucho. "He's the fellow we'd like you to collaborate with." He went on to explain; Johnstone, like myself a comic artist and a staff member of the *Evening World*, was the author of "I'll Say She Is," a boisterous vaudeville sketch which the Marxes had amplified into their first Broadway success. "Yes siree," he concluded somberly. "I can't imagine two people worse equipped for the job, but there's one thing in your favor. You're both such tyros you might just come up with something fresh."

It was a dubious basis for any undertaking, and yet, as events proved, his words had a certain perverse logic. Johnstone turned out to be a jovial, exuberant chap in his late fifties, a raconteur with a fund of newspaper stories. We put in a couple of enjoyable sessions that got nowhere, except for a misty notion that the Marxes might be characterized as stowaways aboard an ocean liner. On the day designated to report our progress, the two of us met outside the Astor, resolved to confess our inadequacy and throw in the towel. Luncheon with the troupe was as disorganized as my colleague predicted it would be. Groucho expatiated at length on his stock-market losses, Chico kept jumping up to place telephone bets, and Harpo table-hopped all over the dining room, discomposing any attractive lady who gave him a second glance. Finally, the issue could be postponed no longer, and Johnstone, courageously assuming the burden, divulged the sum total of our conferences. To our stupefaction, it evoked hosannas.

"Listen," said Groucho, after a whispered colloquy with his brothers. "You fellows have stumbled on something big. This isn't any fly-by-night radio serial—it's our next picture!"

Primed for a totally opposite reaction, Johnstone and I surveyed him speechless; we had expected to be pistol-whipped and summarily flung into Times Square, and in our humility, thought he was being ironical. Within the next half hour, the brothers dispelled any doubt of their enthusiasm. Pinioning our arms, they hustled us across the street into the office of Jesse Lasky, the head of Paramount Pictures. There was a short, confused interval brim-full of references to astronomical sums of money, contracts, and transportation to the Coast, inexplicably for our wives as well. We were to entrain for Hollywood within the week, it was tempestuously agreed, to write the screenplay. The Marxes, scheduled to terminate their Broadway run in a fortnight, were off to London for an engagement at the Palladium, after which they would return to California to shoot our film. When Johnstone and I reeled out into what was now truly the Gay White Way, our faces had the ecstatic, incredulous look of prospectors who had just blundered across the Lost Dutchman Mine.

The delirium of leavetaking for California was, of course, punctuated by the usual untoward incidents that complicate life at such moments. My wife—deliberately, I felt at the time—slipped on an icy sidewalk and fractured her arm, and Johnstone, an undisguised foe of Prohibition, was suddenly disheartened by rumors that applejack was unprocurable in Los Angeles. Solutions materialized for both dilemmas; at the

eleventh hour, my consort was able to board the Twentieth
Century encased in a cast, and influential friends of Johnstone's
mercifully supplied him with three stone crocks of his life-giving
ichor. To further restrict our mobility, we took with us our pet
of the moment, a large and aggressive schnauzer whose antipathy
to trainmen and porters kept the compartment in an uproar.
He was eventually exiled to the baggage car, where he ululated
for three thousand miles and spread neurasthenia among the
postal clerks. Much more awesome than any scenery we saw on
the trip, it developed, was Johnstone's creative drive. In less
than sixty-five hours, he dashed off fifteen or twenty strip
cartoons for his paper, not to mention innumerable water-colors
of the sunsets, mesas, and hogans en route. How his hand remained sufficiently steady, considering the roadbed of the Santa
Fe and the contents of the three stone crocks, was a mystery. I
sometimes lay awake in my berth for as long as two minutes
pondering it.

Of all the world's storied thoroughfares, it must be confessed
that none produces quite the effect of Hollywood Boulevard. I
have been downcast in Piccadilly, chopfallen on the Champs
Elysées, and *doloroso* on the Via Veneto, but the avenues themselves were blameless. Hollywood Boulevard, on the contrary,
creates an instant and malign impression in the breast of the
beholder. Viewed in full sunlight, its tawdriness is unspeakable;
in the torrential downpour of the rainy season, as we first saw it,
it inspired an anguish similar to that produced by the engravings
of Piranesi. Our melancholy deepened when the mem and I took
an exploratory walk around the hotel. As we sat in a Moorish
confectionery patterned after the Alcázar, toying with viscid
malted milks and listening to a funereal organ rendition of
"Moonlight in Kalua," the same thought occurred to each of us,
but she phrased it first.

"Listen," she said. "Do we really need the money this much?"

"That's cowardice," I said, vainglorious because I had held
my tongue. "Why, we just got here—you can't judge a place so
fast. Besides, it's raining. It's probably beautiful when the sun
comes out."

"It's no such thing," she retorted. "You're whistling in the dark, and you know it. It's the Atlantic City boardwalk—a hayseed's idea of the Big Apple. We've made a terrible mistake."

"Oh, we have, have we?" I shouted. Two or three cadavers near us startled out of their torpor turned to survey me, but I didn't care. "Well, you're certainly a comfort. Here we are in the mecca of show business, the paradise everyone dreams about, with one foot on the golden ladder—"

"Unscramble your metaphors," she interrupted coldly. "This town's already beginning to affect you."

"Well, you don't have to sprinkle weed killer over our hopes the first day," I said sulkily. "You could fake a little optimism."

"O.K.," she said, assuming an insincere metallic smile. "No more crabbing. Maybe it's that dismal hotel room of ours that got me down—let's go find a cheerful nest somewhere and start acting like forty-niners."

The bivouac we ultimately settled into, a modest duplex in a bungalow court, had only one advantage—it was new. Otherwise, it was an unalloyed horror, from its overstuffed suite to its painted bedsteads, from its portable gas heaters to its garish dinette. Seated there of an evening over our avocado salads while the radio tinkled out commercials for high-colonics, crematoriums, and sculptured broadlooms, one had the sense of living in a homemaker's magazine. After a few days, I could have sworn that our faces began to take on the hue of Koda-chromes, and even the dog, an animal used to bizarre surroundings, developed a strange, off-register look, as if he were badly printed in overlapping colors. Our neighbors were the customary hodgepodge—studio technicians, old ladies studying Bahai, bit players, chippies, and all the mysterious lamisters who tenant the Los Angeles substratum. They rarely emerged from their burrows, but once in a while we could hear upraised voices extolling the virtues of various faith healers or laxatives. Country people in general display a preoccupation with their innards bordering on the religious, and in Los Angeles, a metropolis made up of innumerable Midwestern hamlets, it amounted to a fixation. Apart from dry cleaners, saddleries, and stores that eternalized baby shoes in bronze, almost every shop in the district was a health-food depot. I have no figures on the per-capita consumption, in Southern California during the early thirties, of soy bean, wheat germ, and blackstrap molasses, and I am thankful. It was frightening.

At the studio, where Johnstone and I were now daily applying ourselves to the script, another and equally fanciful atmosphere prevailed. The two of us were quartered in a ramshackle warren of tan stucco that housed thirty or forty other scribes. They were all in various stages of gestation, some spawning gangster epics and horse operas, others musical comedies, dramas, and farces. Few of them were writers in the traditional sense, but persuasive, voluble specialists adept in contriving trick plot situations. Many had worked before the advent of dialogue, in silent pictures; they viewed the playwrights, novelists, and newspapermen who were beginning to arrive from New York as usurpers, slick wordmongers threatening their livelihood, and rarely fraternized. My collaborator and I, however, had little time to promote social contacts, for a managerial eye was fixed on us to ensure that the script would be forthcoming on time. Herman Mankiewicz, our supervisor, was a large, Teutonic individual with an abrasive tongue, who had been a well-known journalist and *The New Yorker*'s first dramatic critic. Though he was married into the Hollywood hierarchy, his fondness for cards and good living kept him in a state of perpetual peonage and had made him a sort of Johnsonian figure in the industry. Luckily, his duties as our overseer lay lightly on him. He stressed the fact that we were to proceed as fancy dictated, cynically adding that in any case, the Marxes would keelhaul us.

"They're mercurial, devious, and ungrateful," he said. "I hate to depress you, but you'll rue the day you ever took the assignment. This is an ordeal by fire. Make sure you wear asbestos pants."

Johnstone, whose earlier association with the brothers had left no scars, was inclined to scoff at these sentiments, but several weeks later, an incident occurred that unnerved us both. One morning, we were called to Mr. Lasky's office and shown a cable from the Marxes in London. Stating their disenchantment with us in the most succinct terms, they recommended our instant dismissal and replacement by capable writers. Transfixed, we pointed out to Lasky that nobody thus far had seen a word we'd written. He nodded paternally.

"Don't be upset," he advised, smiling. "Actors, you know—they're all a little unstable. I've already replied. I told them to stick to their vaudeville and we'd worry about the movie end."

Evidently the vaudeville was providing its quota of headaches, because rumors of a very cool reception in England soon drifted back to us. Music-hall audiences were not yet attuned to anarchic comedy, and they saluted the Marxes' whirlwind antics by jeering and pitching pennies onto the stage. Insulated from their problems by a continent and an ocean, however, my collaborator and I continued to peg away at our script. We devised jokes and plot twists so hilarious that we could barely gasp them out to each other; we grovelled with laughter in our lazaret as we invented extravagant puns for Groucho, pantomimic flights and Italian malapropisms for his brothers. Zeppo, the youngest, was never a concern, since he was always cast as the juvenile love interest. His speeches were usually throwaways like "Yes, Father" or song cues on the order of "I think you have the loveliest blue eyes I've ever seen."

Six weeks from the day we had begun work, we were notified that the deadline was looming. The troupe was back in the country and about to converge on Hollywood, and we were to read the screenplay to them, *viva voce*, the following Friday night at the Roosevelt Hotel. We put in some intensive burnishing, though, truth to tell, our handiwork already seemed to us to outshine the Kohinoor. To make it still more acceptable, we decided to salt our pages with as many technical movie phrases as we could, many of which we only half understood. We therefore went over the action line by line, panning, irising down, and dissolving, painstakingly sandwiched in Jackman and Dunning shots, and even, at one point, specified that the camera should vorkapich around the faces of the ballroom guests. Neither of us, of course, had the remotest notion of what this last meant, and it was years before I discovered that it derived from a special-effects genius named Slavko Vorkapich. I still have no idea, between ourselves, whether his technique could be applied with impunity to the human face.

At eight-thirty on the appointed evening, I met Johnstone in the suite reserved for our audition. The onus of reading aloud a 126-page script weighed heavily on both of us, so we flipped a coin and I, to my despair, was elected. Half an hour passed without any sign of the quartet, during which I twice urged my colleague to abandon the whole enterprise and leave by the fire escape, but his dentures were chattering so loudly that he did not hear me. Fifteen minutes later, the first auditors arrived—Papa Marx, the progenitor of the band, accompanied by a fellow pinochle player. Our whiplash, Mankiewicz, turned up next, in company with his brother Joseph, then a rising screenwriter at Paramount. They were followed by Zeppo and his wife, who brought along a stately brace of Afghans they had purchased in England. The dogs had eaten the upholstery of a Packard convertible that afternoon and were somewhat subdued in consequence, but they looked intimidating, and they took up a position near my feet that boded ill. Harpo now strolled in with a couple of blond civilians he had dined with, and close on his heels the Chico Marxes, leading a scrappy wirehaired terrier which immediately tangled with the Afghans. In the midst of the tohu-bohu, Groucho and his wife entered; I supposed that thirteen constituted a quorum and made as if to start, but was told to desist—other guests were due. These, it proved, were three gagmen the Marxes had picked up in transit, each of whom was to furnish japes tailored to their respective personalities. (Zeppo, as indicated earlier, could expect only leavings.) Behind the gagmen came *their* wives, sweethearts, and an unidentifiable rabble I took to be relatives, and last of all several cold-eyed vultures obviously dispatched by the studio. When I counted noses and paws before ringing up the curtain, there were twenty-seven people and five dogs confronting me.

The very apogee of embarrassment, according to Madison Avenue, is to dream oneself in some stylish locale, say Carnegie

Hall, clad in a bra other than Maidenform or a supporter not manufactured by Haines. Had I been wearing either or both that night, I could not have experienced worse panic as I stammered forth the setting of our opus. Destiny, whatever its intentions, had never supplied me with forensic gifts, and my only thespian flight theretofore had been a minor role in a high-school pageant based on Pocahontas. The incredible folly of my position, the temerity of a virgin scenarist hoping to beguile a hardened professional audience, suddenly overtook me. I became faint, and the roar of a mighty cataract like the Zambesi Falls sounded in my ears. Stricken, I turned to Johnstone for succor, but cataleptic fear had seized him too; his face, the color of an eggplant, was contorted in a ghastly, fixed smile like Bartholomew Sholto's in *The Sign of the Four*, and I thought for one horrid moment he was defunct.

"Go ahead, man," said a voice I distantly recognized as Groucho's. "Get a move on. As the donkey said, we're all ears."

Short of committing hara-kiri on the spot, there was nothing to do but comply, so, clearing my throat with a force that loosened the sidelights, I continued. I had not proceeded very far before I began to sense a distinct change in the mood of my listeners. At first it was pliant—indulgent, so to speak—and there was an occasional polite ripple. This soon ceased and they became watchful—not hostile as yet, but wary. It was as if they were girding themselves, flexing for trouble they knew was inevitable. Then, by slow degrees, an attitude of sullen resentment stole into their faces. They had been betrayed, lured away from their klabiatsch and easy chairs by a will-o'-the-wisp promise of entertainment, and they grew vengeful. *Some* of them got vengeful, that is; the majority got sleepy, for by then I had stopped inflecting my voice to distinguish one character from another and had settled into a monotonous lilt like a Hindu chanting the Bhagavad Gita. I spared them nothing— the individual shots, the technical jargon, our colorful descriptions of sets and characters. At times my voice faded away altogether and I whispered endless pages of dialogue to the unheeding air. All the while, Johnstone sat with his eyes fixed alternately on his palms and the ceiling, patently trying to dissociate himself from me. Not once did he or anyone else bid me take respite or a glass of water. The whole room—exclusive of those who were asleep, naturally—was watching a man hang himself with a typewriter ribbon, and not a finger was lifted to save him. When I finally croaked "Fade Out" at the end of my ninety-minute unspectacular, there was no sound except the stertorous breathing of the dogs.

After an aeon, Chico stretched, revolved in his chair, and addressed Groucho. "What do you think?" he growled.

With the deliberation of a diamond cutter, Groucho bit the end off his cigar, and applying a match, exhaled a jet of smoke. "It stinks," he said, and arose. "Come on." As he stalked toward the door, he was engulfed in a wedge of sycophants hissing agreement and post-mortems. In another few seconds, the only occupants of the suite were a pair of forlorn sourdoughs numbed by the realization that the Lost Dutchman Mine was actually fool's gold.

Such was my baptism into the picture business, the glamorous and devil-may-care world of illusion I had envied from childhood. I crept away that night to lick my wounds, convinced that this was Waterloo, that contumely and public disgrace would be our portion forever. Happily, I was wrong; in the scalding light of day, our critics capriciously reversed themselves and decided that traces of our handiwork could be salvaged. It took five months of drudgery and Homeric quarrels, ambuscades, and intrigues that would have shamed the Borgias, but it finally reached the cameras, and the end product was *Monkey Business*, a muscular hit. I read the New York reviews in the most ideal surroundings imaginable—a café terrace at Bandol on the Côte d'Azur, midway between Marseilles and Toulon. A soft inshore breeze stirred my wife's hair, a Chambéry *fraise* waited at my elbow, and the schnauzer snored contentedly at our feet. Far more blissful, though, was the certainty that there wasn't a frosted papaya or a sneak preview within a thousand miles.

Even that prince of porcupines, Thoreau, couldn't have asked
for more than that.

My own relationship with Groucho was, in a sense, a baffling
one. I loved his lightning transitions of thought, his ability to
detect pretentiousness and bombast, and his genius for disem-
bowelling the spurious and hackneyed phrases that litter one's
conversation. And I knew that he liked my work for the printed
page, my preoccupation with clichés, baroque language, and the
elegant variation. Nevertheless, I sensed as time went on that
this aspect of my work disturbed him; he felt that some of the
dialogue I wrote for him was "too literary." He feared that
many of my allusions would be incomprehensible to the
ordinary moviegoer, whom he regarded as a wholly cretinous
specimen.

"What'll this mean to the barber in Peru?" he was wont to
complain whenever he came across a particularly fanciful reference. The barber, in his mind, was a prototypical figure—not a
South American, but a Midwestern square in Peru, Indiana,
whose funny bone the Marxes sought to tickle. Groucho visualized him, exhausted from his day's work and attended by a
wife and five children, staring vacuously at the screen and
resenting japes he could not understand. I tried to convince
Groucho that his comedy was unique, a kaleidoscope of parody,
free association, and insult, but he brushed me aside. "That's
O.K. for the Round Table at the Algonquin," he said impatiently. "Jokes—that's what I need. Give me jokes."

The producer charged with supervising *Horsefeathers*, as it
happened, was the same awesome figure who had guided the
destinies of *Monkey Business*, Herman Mankiewicz. The choice,
I suspect, was a deliberate one on the part of Paramount's front
office, for it needed a tough foreman to ride herd on our
anarchical troupe. Mankiewicz, whose stormy Teutonic character and immoderate zest for the grape and gambling have since
been well delineated in connection with the authorship of
Citizen Kane, was a brilliant man, but if he had any lovable

qualities, he did his best to conceal them. He had a tongue like a rasp, and his savage wit demolished anyone unlucky enough to incur his displeasure. I myself was the recipient on various occasions, but one, which Groucho delighted to recall many years later, deserves repetition.

On a very hot midday in July, it seemed, Mankiewicz betook himself to a celebrated restaurant in Hollywood named Eddie Brandstetter's, much frequented by gourmands, where he treated his palate to two whiskey sours and a Gargantuan lunch consisting of lentil soup with frankfurters, rinderbrust with spaetzle, red cabbage and roast potatoes, and noodle pudding, irrigating the mixture with three or four flagons of Pilsener. Then, eyeballs protruding, he lumbered painfully to his car and drove to his office at Paramount. Thrusting aside the handful of messages his secretary extended, he enjoined her not to admit any callers, however importunate, for the next couple of hours and retired into his private sanctum. With the Venetian blinds tightly drawn, he stretched out on a sofa, shielded his face with a copy of the *Hollywood Reporter*, and sank into a blissful snooze.

Barely ten minutes later, he was awakened by a timid, re peated knocking at the door. Mankiewicz's face, mottled with perspiration and mounting fury, swelled like a sunfish as he sat up, prepared to decapitate whoever had flouted his express orders.

"Who the hell is it?" he shouted. "Come in, damn you!"

Two pale-faced young men, twitching with fright, entered haltingly. They were Arthur Sheekman, a gagman Groucho had imported to assist with his material, and myself, and luckless as always, I had been nominated to voice our petition.

"I—I'm sorry to intrude," I began, "but the fact is—the truth of the matter—"

"What the devil do you want?" Mankiewicz barked. "Get the marbles out of your mouth!"

"Well, it's like this," I squeaked, moistening my lips. "In this sequence we're working on, we're kind of perplexed about the identity of the Marx Brothers—the psychology of the characters they're supposed to represent, so to speak. I mean, who *are* they? We—we wondered if you could analyze or define them for us."

"Oh, you did, did you?" he grated. "O.K., I'll tell you in a word. One of them is a guinea, another a mute who picks up spit, and the third an old Hebe with a cigar. Is that all clear, Beaumont and Fletcher? Fine," he concluded, forcing a poisonous smile. "Now get back to your hutch, and at teatime I'll send over a lettuce leaf for the two of you to chew on. Beat it!"

Nathanael West

If, in the latter half of 1932, you were a Midwestern music student at Juilliard, a fledgling copywriter with a marginal salary, or a divorcée rubbing along on a small alimony, the chances are that you lived at one time or another at the Hotel Sutton on East Fifty-sixth Street. The Sutton was a fairly characteristic example of the residential, or soi-disant "club," hotel designed for respectable young folk pursuing a career in New York. There was nothing in the least clublike about it, and it was residential only in the sense that it was an abode, a roof over one's head. Otherwise, it was an impersonal sixteen-story barracks with a myriad of rooms so tiny that their walls almost impinged on each other, a honeycomb full of workers and drones in the minimum cubic footage required to avert strangulation. The décor of all the rooms was identical—fireproof Early American, impervious to the whim of guests who might succumb to euphoria, despair, or drunkenness. The furniture was rock maple, the rugs rock wool. In addition to a bureau, a stiff wing chair, a lamp with a false pewter base, and an end table, each chamber contained a bed narrow enough to discourage any thoughts of venery. As a further sop to respectability, the sexes had been segregated on alternate floors, but the elevator men did not regard themselves as housemothers, and for the frisky, a rear stairway offered ready access or flight. The waitresses in the coffee shop on the ground floor wore peach-colored uniforms and served a thrifty club breakfast costing sixty-five cents. You

161

had a choice of juice—orange or tomato—but not of the glass it came in, which was a heavy green goblet. The coffee, it goes without saying, was unspeakable.

By definition, the manager of the premises should have been a precise, thin-lipped martinet with a cold eye who slunk around counting towels and steaming open the clientele's mail. In point of fact, he was an amiable and well-spoken young man named Nathanael West, whose major interest was books rather than innkeeping. Since I was his friend and brother-in-law, it was only natural that my wife and I gravitated to his hostel when *Sherry Flip* slid into the vortex. A relative with a surplus of rooms was a mighty welcome spar, and we clung to him gratefully. He fixed up two cubbyholes into the semblance of a suite, for which, unsurprisingly, we paid skeletal rates, and he was quick to apply financial poultices when the wolf nipped at our heels. His nepotism, in a way, was an outgrowth of his of situation, for he had been appointed manager by some remote uncle who owned the building. Literary tastes and executive talent rarely go hand in hand, but West, curiously enough, was good at his job. He had charm and a quick sense of humor, as well as an innate sympathy with the problems of his guests. This did not blind him to their deficiencies, nevertheless, and he often confided accounts of eccentric, and indeed clinical, behavior that suggested Dostoyevsky and Krafft-Ebing. He also gave us an insight into the sordid mechanics of operating a metropolitan hotel—the furtive inspection of baggage and letters, the surveillance of guests in arrears, the complex technique of locking out deadheads or impounding their effects, and similar indignities. I presume all of these were perpetuated on us in principle, even though we were kinsmen of the boss, but so subtly that we never caught on.

Had West dreamt of becoming a Conrad Hilton, he would have devoted his spare time to studying cost accounting or new methods of adulterating the coffee. The status of Boniface, however, increasingly irked him. He had never given up the hope of writing professionally, and in such leisure as he could contrive, was working on a second novel. It had its origin in a series of letters shown him several years earlier by a friend of ours, a lady who ran an advice-to-the-lovelorn column on the *Brooklyn Eagle*. For all their naïveté and comic superficialities, the letters were profoundly moving. They dealt with the most painful dilemmas, moral and physical, and West saw in them and their recipient the focus of the story he called *Miss Lonelyhearts*. From its inception to the final version, the book occupied him almost four years. He worked slowly and laboriously; he had none of the facility of the hack writer, the logorrhea with which so many second-rate novelists cloak their shortcomings. He openly disliked the swollen dithyrambs and Whitmanesque fervors of orgiasts like Thomas Wolfe, and the clumsy, unselective naturalism of the proletarian school typified by James Farrell repelled him equally. His chief orientation, as is apparent, was European. Among the Russians, Turgenev, Chekhov, and especially Gogol, with his mixture of fantastic humor and melancholy, appealed to him. He idolized Joyce, considering him, as most of us did, the foremost comic writer in the language, and was strongly attracted to the French surrealists like Aragon, Soupault, and Breton, whose experiments were appearing in *transition*. Along with his avant-gardist flair, there was a deep strain of the conventional in West's nature. He loved custom-tailored clothes—his tailor bills were astronomical—first editions, and expensive restaurants. He fancied himself a Nimrod and fisherman, largely, I often suspected because of the colorful gear they entailed. His taste in women, with whom he tended to be shy, was catholic enough, but he preferred tall, rangy girls who had attended certain finishing schools and universities, the type our generation called snakes. For a brief interval, he even owned a red Stutz Bearcat, until it burst into flames and foundered in a West Virginia gorge. He liked to think of himself as an all-around man.

It is axiomatic that when a couple of bibliophiles meet over a remainder bin, a little magazine always results. During the spring of 1931, West, an inveterate browser, became acquainted with William Carlos Williams at a West Forty-seventh Street bookshop. In a short while their union was blessed by issue—

that is to say, the first one of a quarterly called *Contact*, which they coedited with Robert McAlmon. The title page bore the defiant epigraph "*Contact* will attempt to cut a trail through the American jungle without the aid of a European compass," but the undergrowth must have proved too thick, because the editors shortly switched their policy from geography to merit. They extracted essays from Diego Rivera and Marsden Hartley, as well as contributions from e. e. cummings, Erskine Caldwell, George Milburn, and Ben Hecht (and with due modesty, of course, from themselves). The magazine published four or five numbers, and then, stricken by the anaemia that dogs all such enterprises, a total lack of advertising, folded.

Though West was left with bales of unsolicited manuscripts which eventually stoked the furnace, he did get to know a horde of writers during his editorial tenure, and many of them, trading on his largesse, dossed down at the Sutton on their visits to New York. At teatime the lobby frequently took on the air of Yaddo or a book-and-author luncheon. Burly, pipe-smoking poets with thick orange cravats—nobody has yet ascertained why poets affect neckwear that has the texture of caterpillars—stood around swapping metres with feverish lady librarians from the Dakotas; the girl at the newsstand who sold you the sports final, unless you were quick on your feet, would try to read you a quatrain in the manner of Rimbaud. One evening, as I was descending alone in the elevator, the operator, a cretin I was certain I had never seen before, halted his car between floors and turned to me with a businesslike gleam in his eye. I thought he was about to glom my stickpin and leave through the escape hatch, but when he spoke, it was in the rich Stanislavskian cadence of a Group Theatre actor.

"Excuse me, sir," he said deferentially. "The housekeeper told me you had a big hit on Broadway. I'm scripting a play too, on a Biblican theme, but I got stuck in the second act, in the obligatory scene. Could you recommend a good book or construction, or would you advise me to go back to the Bible?"

I advised him, and thereafter used the stairs. Not all the aspiring writers at the Sutton, however, were slated for anonymity. Lillian Hellman, whom I had originally met when she was a reader for Horace Liveright and married to Arthur Kober, was holed up there, struggling with her first solo effort, *The Children's Hour*. A pallid youth on the third floor, named Norman Krasna, hitherto a flack in the Warner Brothers publicity department, was endlessly retyping Hecht and MacArthur's *The Front Page*, hoping to learn something of dramatic structure. His toil eventuated in a clamorous comedy on public relations that left Broadway unmoved but swept him on to Hollywood and affluence. The one writer of celebrity in the establishment was something of a recluse. This was Dashiell Hammett, who, in the pages of magazines like *Black Mask* and four novels, had revolutionized the whole concept of police fiction. Like most innovators, he had reaped small financial benefit from his work and was on a lee shore. He had been living, prior to his arrival in our midst, at an opulent Fifth Avenue hotel where he had run up a whopping bill. Unable to pay it, he was forced, in English parlance, to "shoot the moon" and abscond with as many of his belongings as he could conceal. His knowledge of the mentality of house detectives provided the key. A tall, emaciated man easily identifiable in a crowd, Hammett decided to use fat as a subterfuge. He pulled on four shirts, three suits, innumerable socks, two lightweight ulsters, and an overcoat, cramming his pockets with assorted toiletries. Then he puffed out his cheeks, strode past the desk without a glimmer of suspicion, and headed for the Sutton, whose manager was acquiring kudos among literary folk as a Good Samaritan. West, a clotheshorse himself, recognized in Hammett a sartorial genius. He put him on the cuff and staked him to a typewriter and a bottle of beer a day. The upshot, the best-seller called *The Thin Man*, clinched Hammett's reputation.

It was another pen pal of West's, in this same seedy epoch, who sweet-talked him into a venture that addled our brains for years to come. About mid-autumn of 1932, my wife and I began to detect glowing references in her brother's speech to Bucks County, Pennsylvania. He had latterly been weekending there with Josephine Herbst, the novelist, and his accounts of the flora, the architecture, and the natives verged on the rhapsodic. Owing to its remoteness and the paucity of highways, the district was still altogether rural; but the submarginal land and the inroads of the Depression had brought about a wave of farm foreclosures, and property was ridiculously cheap. Inevitably, West conceived a romantic dream of ourselves as country squires. He visualized us cantering on fat cobs through leafy lanes, gloating over our waving fields of alfalfa, the great stone barns decorated with hex signs, and the lowing kine. He saw himself as a mighty shikar stalking through pheasant cover, gun dogs at his heels, clad in all the corduroy vests and bush jackets he had lusted for endlessly at Abercrombie's. Since I was stony at the moment, eroded by debt and hostile to any prospect of becoming a mortgagee, West started a campaign of suasion that was a masterpiece of sophistry. The Revolution, he pointed out, was imminent; how sensible it would be for us, when "La Carmagnole" rang across the barricades, to own a patch of ground where we could raise the necessities of life. Fish and game were so abundant in the Delaware Valley that shad, rabbits, and quail had to be restrained from leaping into the cook pot. If Roosevelt closed the banks as predicted, we could grow our own tobacco, cobble our shoes with tough, fragrant birch bark. He painted a pastorial of the three of us in our bee-loud glade, my wife contentedly humming as she bottled raspberry jam, he and I churning out an unending stream of prose. Where the requisite paper would come from, since we were to dispense with cash, he did not specify. Doubtless he expected the forest to supply it.

I turned a deaf ear to all such blandishments, but his sister, who was easier to influence, succumbed. One Monday morning, the two of them returned from a reconnaissance of the section pale with excitement. They had stumbled across the ultimate, the *ne plus ultra*, in farmsteads—an eighty-seven-acre jewel in the rolling uplands bordering the river. Their voices shook as they described the stone house on a hillside circumscribed by a tumbling creek, the monumental barn above larger than the cathedral at Chartres. The place, it appeared, belonged to a left-wing journalist, one Mark Silver, who had tried to launch a ne'er-do-well brother in the chicken business there. The brother and other rodents had eaten the fowls, and Silver, to compound his troubles, was involved with a tigress in New York who was threatening a breach-of-promise suit. To enable him to flee to Mexico, which seemed to him an ideal solution for his woes, he was willing to accept a token payment for the farm, plus easy installments. In West's view, it was the biggest steal since the theft of the *Mona Lisa* from the Louvre.

I grudgingly went out with them to see the place, and in a trice also fell for it. The autumn foliage was at its height, and the woods and fields blazed with color. In contrast to the bedlam of New York, the only sound that disturbed the sylvan hush was the distant chatter of crows in the north forty. There was an air of permanence, of solidity, about the house and outbuildings that captivated and reassured. My glasses steamed over as a series of colored lantern slides flashed before me—sleigh rides, Hallowe'en parties, sugaring off, sugaring on, and bringing in the Yule log. We hastened through the dwelling, exclaiming over virtues like its massive fireplaces and deep window reveals and conveniently ignoring its drawbacks. Bathrooms, engineered kitchens, and oil furnaces bloomed in our overheated imagination; magically, we became a trio of Paul Bunyans, shearing off porches, cementing cellars, and relocating stone partitions. Sound as the house was, we had to admit that the previous tenants had left it in parlous condition. The living-room closet was heaped with empty walnut husks, and judging from the pots and dishes on the stove, the residents had departed as precipitately as the crew of the *Marie Celeste*. A tour of the farm buildings disclosed that Silver's brother, following the poultry debacle, had turned his hand to cabinetmaking. The sheds were piled with dozens of modernistic plywood bookcases, striped in bronze radiator paint and hot tropical colors. The monstrous things harassed me for years afterward; whenever I tried to chop them up for fireplace use, the fibrous, springy wood repelled the axe and perforated me with splinters. I eventually made an apocalyptic bonfire of them, nearly burning down the barn in the process.

Several years later, incidentally, I learned that a celebrated colleague had seen the property and its owners, just before we did, under peculiarly harrowing circumstances. George S. Kaufman was being shown some of the real estate available in the neighborhood, Kaufman strenuously protesting the while to his wife that he detested the out-of-doors, that country living was full of pitfalls, and that nobody had ever incurred a hernia in Reuben's. Up at the Silver Farm, as they ascended its winding lane, a lesson in firearms was in progress: Mark Silver, who could not open an umbrella without puncturing someone's lung, was initiating his brother in the mysteries of handling a shotgun.

"They call this the breech," he explained, opening the mechanism. "We place the bullet, or shell, in there. Then we close it, like so, and raising it to the shoulder, aim along the barrel and squeeze here."

He pressed the trigger smartly, unaware that the weapon was still trained on his brother's foot. Simultaneously with the explosion, the Kaufmans materialized as though on cue, just in time to see the hapless brother bite the dust. Silver stared at the casualty, his face contorted in horror, and then bounded up to the arrivals.

"Cain and Abel!" he bellowed, and smote his forehead. "Woe is me—I have slain my own brother!"

Kaufman took off like an impala, and it was a decade before he would consent to enter even Central Park. Had West and I had any such therapeutic experience, we too might have been cured of our obsession; but the poison was circulating in our veins, and a fortnight afterward, in a simple ceremony at the county courthouse, two blushing innocents were married to four score and seven acres. Raising my half of the five-hundred-dollar deposit baffled us until my wife came up with a brilliant expedient. The one piano at the Sutton, she suggested, was quite inadequate for the Juilliard scholars, who required sustained practice. She and I had a baby grand in storage, an heirloom from her family, which we might be willing to sacrifice for a consideration in a worthy cultural cause. Her brother went into some pretty complex double-talk with the owners of the hotel to justify his expenditure of two hundred and fifty dollars, but they ultimately held still for it. After all, as West fluently pointed out, he had single-handedly transformed the joint from a flophouse into an artistic mecca.

For the next couple of months, every ounce of energy the three of us could summon—along with whatever paint, hardware, tools, and furniture West could liberate from the hotel short of downright larceny—went into making the farm habitable. The self-deceit of landowners is proverbial, but we reached new heights; we became artisans as well, installing pumps and plumbing, wiring the house, and even, in a Herculean spurt that left us crippled for weeks, implanting a septic tank. All these furbelows, being makeshift, constantly tended to remind us of our inadequacy. Water pipes we had painstakingly soldered would burst their seams in the middle of the night, with a roar like Krakatoa, and drench us in our beds. Tongues of blue fire licked at our homemade electrical conduits; half the time we reeled about with catastrophic headaches, unaware that the furnace needed escape vents to discharge its burden of coal gas. Each weekend was a turmoil of displacement. Groaning like navvies, we trundled barrows of shale to and fro, unrooted and redistributed trees, realigned fences, and change the entire topography of the place. The vogue for Pennsylvania Dutch artifacts had not yet become general, and there were quantities of dough trays, dry sinks, horsehair sofas, Victorian wig stands, and similar rubbish available around the county to any fool who confused himself with Chippendale. We invariably did, and spent endless nights in a haze of shellac dust, scraping away at some curlicued gumwood commode to bring out the beauty of the grain.

Spring was upon us with a rush of seed catalogues, and we were about to occupy our demesne and see if we could subsist on tomatoes, when the wheel of fortune took an unexpected spin. The Marx Brothers besought me to go West and fashion

another movie for them, *Horsefeathers,* this time in collaboration with Kalmar and Ruby, the songwriters. Somewhat less
than radiant at the thought of being sucked into the millrace a
second time, I hesitated, but the long financial drought had
sapped my resistance. At almost the same time, West's novel
Miss Lonelyhearts was published to considerable critical acclaim.
Its early promise of sales, unhappily, was blasted by the publisher's bankruptcy, and though another firm soon reissued it,
the delay was fatal. There was, however, a small silver lining.
The film rights were acquired for a handful of lima beans by
Darryl Zanuck (who, parenthetically, transmutted it into a tepid
comedy), and it was on the proceeds that West decided to chuck
his job and devote himself to full-time authorship.

Our farewell to him at the farm, where he was starting to
woo his muse with a few Spartan adjuncts like an inkhorn, a
14-gauge shotgun, and a blooded pointer, took place in an
atmosphere of mingled resignation and hope. It seemed a cruel
irony to be cheated of the rustic joys we had labored to achieve,
and yet, if we were ever to enjoy them, a spell in the Hollywood
deep freeze was unavoidable. As for West, his mood was
jubiliant; he was through forever with the hotel business, with
pettifogging bookkeepers and commission merchants, with the
neurotics, drunks, and grifters he had been called on to comfort
and wheedle. He had two tangible licenses to hunt and to fish,
and one, invisible, to starve as a free-lance writer. We toasted
his future and ours with a gulp of forty-rod, and bidding him
Godspeed, turned our faces to the setting sun.

Dorothy Parker

Dorothy Parker was already a legend when I first met her in the autumn of 1932. Her bittersweet verses and dialogues, her *bon mots*, and her love affairs had made her a distinctive figure in the group of journalists and playwrights who congregated at the Algonquin for lunch and at Tony's, Jack & Charlie's, and the Stork Club for more extended liquefaction. The way in which we met was not one I would have chosen—in fact, it was a scarifying ordeal—but since we ultimately became friends and neighbors, it is worth narrating if only as indicative of manners and customs in the Prohibition era.

The occasion was a cocktail party given by Poultney Kerr, the bibulous producer of *Sherry Flip*, the revue I had written some sketches for and which was about to begin rehearsal. The show at that point lacked a title, and Kerr, seizing on any pretext for a bash, invited forty or fifty social and theatrical acquaintances to drinks at his office in the hope that someone would come up with a frisky and forceful name for the enterprise. Halfway through the proceedings Mrs. Parker arrived, visibly gassed but dressed to kill in a black confection by Lanvin, a feathered toque, and opera-length gloves. Thirty-nine years old and a very toothsome dish, she immediately made every other woman in the assemblage feel dowdy, and for a moment the sound of their teeth gnashing drowned out the buzz of chitchat. When Kerr introduced us, she straightaway fired off a barrage of compliments likening me to Congreve, Oscar Wilde, and Noël Coward.

Inasmuch as my total Broadway output was confined to one sketch in the *Third Little Show*, I thought the praise a mite excessive, but I blushingly accepted the tribute. Having fortified the company with several rounds of malt, Kerr called for silence, explained the purpose of the gathering, and bade everyone don his thinking cap. Needless to say, all heads turned toward Mrs. Parker, who accepted the challenge.

"Let me see," she pondered. "What about *Sing High, Sing Low*? No, that's defeatist. It needs something frothy, sparkling —wait, I know! *Pousse-Café*!"

There was an all but imperceptible ripple, and several willowy young men murmured, "Splendid . . . Yes, definitely . . . Oh, I love it." In the hush that followed, I suddenly became aware of Mrs. Parker's eyes fixed on me with catlike intentness. "What do *you* think of *Pousse-Café*, Mr. Perelman?"

"Great!" I said, striving to put conviction into my tone. "It's gay and—and sparkling, you're right. But it lacks—how shall I say?—punch. I mean, *poose*-café—it's too soft, somehow."

"Oh, really?" she asked, with a slow and deadly inflection. "Well, then, here's something punchier. How about *Aces Up*?"

"*Aces Up*," I mused. "That's marvellous, very good. I just wonder, though, if we can't find something a *tiny* bit sharper, less static . . ."

"Well, goodness me." Mrs. Parker's words dripped sweet poison. "What ever shall we do? Our wrist has just been slapped by the house genius there, who feels that we're a bit dull-witted. Of course, *he's* in a position to know, isn't he, leaning down from Parnassus—"

"Look, folks!" Kerr broke in nervously. "Have another drink. Don't go, it's still early—"

"How privileged we are to have the benefit of Mr. P.'s wide experience!" she overrode him. "How gracious of him to analyze our shortcomings! I wonder, though, if Mr. P. realizes that he's a great big etcetera. Because he is, you know. In fact, of all the etceteras I've ever known—"

Well, fortunately for me, the bystanders who had witnessed the carnage recovered their tongues at this juncture, and the rest of Mrs. Parker's diatribe was lost in the babble. I made my escape, and when Kerr phoned me the next day to apologize for her conduct, I swore that if I ever met the woman again, I'd skewer her with one of her own hatpins. That evening I received a dozen magnificent roses from her accompanied by a note steeped in remorse. It was the beginning of a friendship that survived the next thirty-five years, with intermittent lapses. When my wife and I saw her again on the Coast, she was married to Alan Campbell and from all outward appearances was prosperous. The two worked successfully as screenwriters (and in fact I collaborated with them on a film at M-G-M several years later) and might have continued except that Dottie detested Hollywood. Laura and I, who shared her feeling, spoke often of our place in Bucks County; we tended to become lyrical about the countryside, the farmhouses, and the relative simplicity of life there, and evidently our encomiums had an effect. In time we began to notice the recurrence in Dottie's speech of the word "roots."

"We haven't any roots, Alan," she would admonish him after the fourth Martini. "You can't put down any roots in Beverly Hills. But look at Laura and Sid—they've got *roots*, a place to come home to. Roots, roots."

It was practically foreordained, hence, that a month or two after we settled down at our place, the Campbells suddenly materialized on the doorstep with shining faces. They were surfeited with the artificiality and tinsel of Hollywood, they declared; they wanted a farm near ours and they wanted us to help them find it. Property was still cheap in our area, though farther down the Delaware around New Hope, George S. Kaufman, Moss Hart, and several other playwrights had acquired houses and Bucks County was becoming known as a haunt of writers and artists. Dottie and Alan, however, were imbued with what might be called the creative spirit. Not for them a manor house equipped with creature comforts like bathrooms, stainless steel kitchens, and laundries. They wanted a place that had "possibilities", something they would have fun remodeling. It was clearly an assignment for Jack Boyle.

Jack Boyle was a stage Irishman, straight out of George McManus's comic strip, one of the cronies Jiggs was forever hobnobbing with at Dinty Moore's and incurring Maggie's wrath. He was by way of being a real-estate agent, though he spent a good deal of his time seated on the steps of our local post office telling yarns. In a sense, Jack was one of the most celebrated personages in the district, even if nobody there knew it, for his exploits were immortalized in a book called *The Professional Thief* published by the University of Chicago. He had specialized in stealing furs from department stores, employing a technique that baffled the New York police authorities for years. It was his practice to enter a store, just prior to closing, attired in a balmacaan or similar loose topcoat, and to secrete himself in one of the pay toilets. After the store's watchman had made his rounds, Boyle would hasten to the ladies' fur coat section, select a particularly valuable mink or broadtail garment, and return to his cubicle. Soon after the establishment opened the next morning, he would emerge wearing the loot under his coat and stroll off. The truly extraordinary feature of his caper, though, was that he always turned over the money given him by the fence to a cause he believed in: he was a philosophical anarchist. Eventually betrayed by an informer, he so confused the police with an explanation of his motives that they sent him to Matteawan, but he managed to escape and ultimately, after extended litigation, to beat the rap. Thereafter, he had changed his venue to our township, where he trucked an occasional load of wood to Greenwich Village or negotiated the sale of a farm.

It was a lead-pipe cinch that anyone with so colorful a background would appeal to Dottie, and the two instantly hit it off. A couple of days thereafter, Laura and I accompanied the Campbells on an inspection tour of several farms that Boyle listed. The second one we saw was such a plum that had our friends hesitated, we ourselves would have snapped it up. The central portion of the house, its two lateral wings, and the summer kitchen extending from it were all built of field stone. Three enormous Norway maples shaded the residence on its north side; on the south was an apple orchard in full bloom.

About fifty yards distant stood a stone barn slightly smaller than Aeolian Hall. The dwelling and its outbuildings, reached by a long lane that guaranteed privacy, lay on a gently rolling southern slope of one hundred twenty acres, and the asking price was four thousand five hundred dollars. As Boyle quoted the figure and all our jaws dropped in unison, he raised his hand.

"A word of advice before you grab it, friends," he told the Campbells. "I think you ought to see the inside first. It needs—well, it needs a little attention."

Even with his warning, none of us was prepared for the actuality. The interior of the house was in an appalling state; floors had rotted out in places, revealing the cellar below, fragments of plaster hung from the ceilings, woodwork gave way at the touch. A disused incubator for baby chicks was balanced crazily in the largest room, and a thick film of poultry feathers and cobwebs shrouded everything. It seemed incredible that the ruin was inhabited, yet, said Boyle, an old Ukrainian couple had been living there several years and cultivating a few fields, thanks to the generosity of the owners.

There is a specially insidious form of self-deception afflicting house hunters wherein they confuse themselves with Hercules, equal to any Augean stable they encounter, and the Campbells promptly succumbed to it. They ran around envisioning the rooms a clever architect could fabricate out of the shell, the baths and bedchambers and butler's pantries necessary for country living, and in all conscience we did nothing to disillusion them, for the prospect of having Dottie as a neighbor was a stimulating one. It did not occur to us that we had taken on the role of midwives, that the Campbells expected us to accouche the birth of their dream house, and that we would be called upon to provide sympathy and counsel—to say nothing of anodynes like Martinis—for the manifold problems plaguing them.

The next few months were a caution. The pair installed themselves at an inn near Doylestown were they groaned through all the legal complexities of acquiring their place, choosing an architect, and approving his plans. Infatuated with him at first, they fell out of love with him in short order; he was stodgy, un-imaginative, old-fashioned. The Ukrainians, who had been given notice to vacate, turned obstinate; they refused to adapt them-selves to the new owners' timetable and hung on, maddening Alan beyond measure. He turned in desperation to Jack Boyle, who pointed out, reasonably enough, that the old people had chickens they were preparing to market, standing crops not yet ready for harvest.

"That's *their* problem," Alan retorted passionately. "Don't they realize it's costing Dottie and me seven hundred and fifty dollars a week to stay away from Hollywood?"

Three Little Photoplays and How They Grew

I

Bestowing the award for the most odious person you ever knew in Hollywood isn't the sort of thing you rush into; you're faced, so to speak, with an embarrassment of riches. I guess on reflection that I'd choose a comedian at Universal I'll call Eddie Buzzard, who perched on my desk all the time I worked there importuning me to make with the yocks. He finally surpassed himself—whipped out a lady's hair comb that he wedged between his lips in a version of the *risus sardonicus*, which terminated my two days at Universal. The choice of the second most odious person, on the other hand, is a cinch: a screenwriter named Jack McGovern. McGovern and I collaborated, in a manner of non-speaking, on the script of *Sittin' Pretty*, a Paramount musical I've miraculously escaped seeing to this day. All I remember is that it starred Jack Oakie and Jack Haley, that it chronicled their backstage rise *per aspera ad astra*, and that its hit song was "Jevva See a Dream Walking?" Don't let any purist tell you the initial words in that title were "Did You." It was "Jevva"—I was right there when its creator, fat, genial wordsmith Mack Gordon of the team of Gordon and Revel, first mumbled it.

The producer of *Sittin' Pretty*, Anatol Crown, was a bouncy hyperthyroid with an explosive laugh, a backslapper who generated an aura of noisy excitement that passed for good-fellowship. At his bungalow office on the Paramount lot, I voiced the ritual falsehood required of all scenarists—namely, that the story verged on genius, that the opportunity to work on it was equivalent to knighthood—and was presented to Mc-Govern, a beefier forerunner of Archie Bunker, all rampant pugnacity and no neck. Consecrating our match under the authority invested in him by the All-Highest, B. P. Schulberg, Crown pledged us not to measure out our talent in coffee spoons but to give of our hearts'-blood if necessary. Later that afternoon, as the two of us sat in the offices we shared rereading the treatment, I felt McGovern's eyes drilling into me. Though we hadn't exchanged a word since our introduction, the hostility he exuded was almost palpable. Unable to think how I'd offended him, I decided at last that Anatol Crown was the heavy. During his locker-room talk, he had enjoined me to pepper the script with plenty of good brittle dialogue. Brittle dialogue, as typified in the comedies of Philip Barry and George Kelly, was much in vogue in 1933, but not with McGovern, who prided himself on being a plot expert, a master constructionist. Indirectly, I had been classified as an aesthete, a bookworm, and probably, in McGovern's fierce tribal code, as a pouf.

Most of the next day, McGovern lurked in his own cubicle, emerging only to stare balefully at me or to dispatch Marie, our secretary, for coffee. Ridiculous and absurd as it was, the fact was inescapable: McGovern was trying to freeze me out, to make me crack under pressure, and I determined to force a showdown. When I came into the office the following morning, though, he was absorbed in dictation to Marie.

"Why, here's Mr. Brittle," he said with sweet venom. "Just get a load of this, Brittle—it's a letter to one of my mother-in-laws."

"I'm not interested in your private affairs," I said with more hauteur than Lord Curzon reviewing a durbar. "What I want is an understanding—"

"And you shall have it, Algernon, the moment I'm through with his," he promised. "Read back, Marie—where was I?"

The body of the letter was short and unencumbered by affection for the addressee. It merely set forth that on emigrating to the Coast he had left in her attic a trunk containing several unproduced plays that he now wished her to forward. They were, admittedly, sophomoric, but he was confident they would fetch big bucks as screen material. He hoped she was well, etc., etc.

"How do I sign off, Mr. McGovern?" Marie asked him. " 'Yours sincerely'? 'Cordially yours'? or what?"

"A good question," he commented. "Sign it 'Your ex-son-in-law' "—he paused in thought—" 'who might still be your son-in-law if a certain party hadn't sat around the Clover Club and Ciro's night after night with every faker and gigolo on the Pacific Slope while the poor simp married to her was slaving away at the studio and then, to top it off, one week after he bought her an Auburn convertible for her birthday she had the gall to file for divorce naming a very lovely person on South Palm Drive that just because the two of them were in pajamas when the dicks broke in . . .' "

The subordinate clause, a page and a half long, rambled into other fragrant episodes of a union as joyless as any I ever heard of in the City of Joyless Unions. Formulating it, though, seemed to have exerted a therapeutic effect on McGovern similar to phlebotomy, cupping him of some of his spleen. Not all, but enough for us to arrange a modus vivendi; to reduce contact with each other to a minimum, we agreed to write alternate sequences of *Sittin' Pretty*. It worked out surprisingly well— even if the combined first draft made no sense at times—because of an unforeseen bit of luck. Anatol Crown's mind, at that juncture, was elsewhere than on the script. He was planning to elope with a starlet named Toby Wing.

We received a clear intimation that drama was brewing at a conference he summoned us to on the fourth of August. I recall the date because it was, of course, the anniversary of the Borden murders in Fall River, an event sempiternal in the memory of Rhode Islanders, and it was the same kind of weather—stifling, humid, unendurable. As McGovern and I, still unspeaking, approached the producer's bungalow, we beheld a striking sight.

Eight long-stemmed American beauties, seated in as many rowing machines on the concrete walkway, were being filmed for a trailer plugging a picture called *Eight Girls in a Boat*. The ladies had been rowing strenuously for three hours in the savage heat and were beat, but the unit director, a perfectionist, was mercilessly demanding fresh takes. It was one of those pastiches of life behind the silver screen that used to cause Sidney Skolsky to choke up and that still evoke Rona Barrett's noblest dithyrambs.

Bright-eyed as a teddy bear, Crown sat at the desk in his knotty-pine office excitedly jabbering into a phone. Gordon and Revel, the songwriting team, or more accurately, teamsters, occupied twin chairs along one wall, and ranged on a davenport along the other were three gagmen named Felsey, Greslow, and Profundo.

"Hi, fellas, be with you in a minute!" Crown called out. "Hello? . . . Who? . . . I was talking to the Thieves' Market in Glendale. . . . Oh, you are—good! Listen, it's about that seventy-six-piece dinner service I bought. You made a mistake—you sent me two extra gravy boats instead of the creamers I ordered. . . . *Creamers!* . . . How should I know how to spell it? . . . No, I haven't got the slip—they never sent me a slip! . . . Well, then look it up, look it up!"

He slammed down the receiver, circled around the desk to shake hands with us warmly, and after a general commendation, brought forth a criticism. We had lost one vital ingredient in the original story, he said—credibility.

"Boys, the central premise in this picture can't miss, and why do I say that?" he asked the room. "I say that because it's pure gold. Oakie and Haley, two talented hoofers stranded in New York, find jobs in a wholesale meat concern trimming sides of beef, unpacking the frozen turkeys, and grading sow bellies. The boss has a beautiful daughter that they flip over, so to win her hand they organize a musical show to celebrate the old man's birthday which builds up into the biggest hit on Broadway. That to me is a dynamite springboard for laughs and entertainment, but somehow you failed to make it believable."

He looked around uncertainly. "Did anyone else have that reaction?"

The gagmen, who through an oversight or because their status was too lowly had not been provided with copies of the script, were handicapped for an answer, but all three felt the story wholly plausible and fraught with paroxysms of mirth. The songsmiths began a long Talmudic analysis of various Broadway hits to demonstrate that logic would have been an impediment, if not downright fatal, to their success. Halfway through it, Lucille, Crown's secretary, appeared in the doorway, signalling urgently.

"Mr. Crown—excuse me! I'm having trouble with those reservations up at you-know-where."

"Sh-h-h!" Aghast at the possibility that she might have disclosed some vital detail of his romance, he bounded over to whisper in her ear. Simultaneously, the phone on his desk rang. "Pick it up, someone!" he appealed. "Can't you see I'm busy?"

I did so. The caller was Irving Hoffman, a columnist on the *Hollywood Reporter* I knew slightly. "What are you doing in Crown's office?" he asked. "Oh, I remember now—we ran an item you were on his musical with that swine, McGovern." I signified that the individual in question was within earshot. "Then pour in some henbane—the whole world will applaud you. Listen, an informant of ours at a store in Glendale says that Anatol's bought a hundred-piece dinner service from them, which could mean he's nesting. What's the score?"

Ere I could confirm or deny, Crown commandeered the phone and shouldered the burden of his own public relations. He was chirruping away to Hoffman, pretending elaborate surprise at the elopement rumors, when a sudden tumult became audible at the bungalow's entrance. Amid a babble of voices, half a dozen people crowded in around a studio grip carrying a recumbent figure: one of the lassies on the rowing machines had fainted. Immediately, everyone in the place became a combination of Sir William Osler and the Mayo Brothers, shouting "Get some water—no, ammonia!," "Put her head lower than her feet!," and similar Aesculapian precepts. The fair oarswoman was placed on the davenport, her forehead was laved and her wrists chafed, and in short order, her coral lips were wreathed in a weak smile. It was at that moment that Anatol Crown, his interview with Hoffman concluded, forced his way through the crush. He stared at the girl dazedly a moment, then knelt down beside her.

"How are you feeling, honey?"

"I—I guess I'll be all right."

"That's good," he said. "Tell me, what do you think of the script so far?"

II

The first time my wife and I worked on the M-G-M lot, we did a four-month stint for the fabled Irving Thalberg, in the fabled Irving Thalberg unit, on a yarn called *Greenwich Village*. A soi-disant original, *Greenwich Village* was possibly the most towering pyramid of clichés ever piled up by the human head, second only to *Bouvard et Pécuchet*, and it cried out for Flaubert to do the screenplay, but Gus was busy dialoguing *Salaambô* over at Twentieth and we drew the assignment. Unfortunately, we never got a clear reading from Mr. Thalberg about whether he wanted *La Vie de Bohème* or another *Rip Tide: The Story of a Woman's Conflicting Emotions* or a singing disaster film like *San Francisco*, so in the end, as the Tarot pack accurately predicted, we went back to Bucks County and he to Elysium. And now, two years later, we were again in Culver City, prepared to weave a tapestry or incise a scrimshaw for Thalberg's acknowledged equal and fellow-Titan, the fabled Hunt Stromberg.

Our first encounter, in the opulent office of his two-story villa, was heartening; the man was incontestably a satrap, as all of them were, but he differed from Thalberg as chalk from cheese. He was a large blond Oklahoman, rather earnest, a bit bland, not at all imperious—he had none of the other's knifelike, tiger-of-the-deep menace. In fact, the candor of his approach did much to establish a rapport between us.

"You know, I've got a confession to make," he said. "I did something that would scandalize most Hollywood producers—I brought you folks out here without a definite property in mind. I said to myself, I said, for once let's find out what ignites people to write—let *them* choose the material that stirs their creative juices, that primes their creative pump—and then give them complete freedom and unlimited time to develop it. How does that strike you?"

The clang of the hammer ridding us of our creative shackles stunned us temporarily, but we managed to stammer out our gratification.

"Fine," he said. "Now, I'm badly in need of a vehicle for two of my stars, William Powell and Luise Rainer. Have you seen anything at all in the theatre, have you read a novel or a short story or whatever that might fit their talents?"

Well, there flashed before me a montage of all the marvelous fictional characters they could play, like Willie Baxter and Lola Pratt in *Seventeen*, Dido and Aeneas, and Tom Sawyer and Becky Thatcher. Still, I speculated, didn't Powell have a bit too much mileage on him to whitewash fences and hide in organ lofts? Luckily, before I had a chance to blurt out any of these ideas, which would have entailed countless technical problems, my wife had a brain wave.

"Do you remember that comedy of the Theatre Guild's that Lunt and Fontanne were in called *At Mrs. Beam's?*" she reminded me. Its locale, she explained to Stromberg, was a London boardinghouse, and the Lunts had played a Brazilian couple, a volatile, jealous pair of adventurers who pummeled each other senseless and disrupted the entire place with their intrigues. Was that the sort of thing he envisioned?

Stromberg glowed. "Sounds like a terrific romp—just what I was hoping for. I'll get hold of it toot sweet and we'll huddle in a day or two."

Thirteen days dragged by, and when he surfaced it was to request that we tell him the plot, he had been too busy to read the play. The detailed recital by two people of a comedy, even if their name be Feydeau, is about as zestful as a dish of cold farina, and Stromberg's reaction was predictable. In a setting devoid of glamour, he said, two Brazilians beating up on each other did not necessarily spell box-office. The transition to his next remark, however, was lightning-fast. Had we perchance ever heard of a play by George Bernard Shaw called *Arms and the Man?* We said we had. What about an operetta called *The Chocolate Soldier?* Yes, that was Oscar Straus' musical version of the Shaw play. Lord love you, Mr. Stromberg, I thought, what in the world can you be getting at? He cut short our suspense in the next breath. Arising with the air of triumph Cagliostro displayed when performing his illusions, he laid his finger slyly alongside his nose.

"I," he announced, "am going to combine the two—*Arms and the Man* and *The Chocolate Soldier.* The wit of Bernard Shaw and the musical genius of Oscar Straus."

When the roaring in her head subsided, my mate found her voice. "This is for William Powell and Luise Rainer?"

"No, no, of course not." He paused theatrically before unveiling his surprise. "For Jeanette MacDonald and Nelson Eddy!"

The two of us sat there, stomachs gripped by the sickening contraction one feels when the elevator plunges twenty stories into the basement. So the honeymoon was over; all that marmalade about the perfect wedding of talent and subject matter was really anaesthesia. What babes in the wood we had been. We should have foreseen that the pastry chef for meringues like *The Firefly, Maytime,* and *Rose Marie* would inevitably spring the Iron Butterfly and the Singing Capon on us. And now, as if things weren't dire enough, Stromberg gave the vise another turn. Dismissing the Shavian mélange, he fastened on Victor Herbert's most emetic operetta, *Sweethearts,* as his final choice— meetings to be held forthwith at which we would savor the music and thresh out the story line.

In reality, what took place was no conference but the most extraordinary solo performance. For the next three days, Stromberg manfully wrestled our common language until he pinned its shoulders to the mat. Pacing up and down and with occasional musical interludes, he dictated to a pair of secretaries a long, Baudelairean prose poem—his conception of the project—for our guidance in forging the screenplay.

"I visualize Nelson in this production as a man's man," it ran in part. "Athletic, a bon vivant, and independently wealthy, he is always to be found where the sporting fancy congregates, such as the Madison Square Garden, the Kentucky Derby, Hialeah, etc. Is there a big track meet, six-day bike race, golf classic, or heavyweight championship fight? Why, there you will find Nelson cheering on the contestants, posting wagers, deeply absorbed in the fray. He knows but little of love and romance, having been raised in Hell's Kitchen where he hewed his way with his fists in sharp contrast to Jeanette's patrician background. She has sprung from an unbroken line stretching back to the *Mayflower*, the crème de la crème bulwarked by money and social position. Dainty, headstrong, impetuous, she is like some gorgeous orchid; she recks not of the morrow, avid to indulge that instant whim which will not be denied. Collide they must, these two strong personalities, producing musical sparks that pour from their throats in Victor Herbert's deathless score."

In affliction of this sort, as Edmond Dantès discovered, one falls back on minutiae for consolation. We found ours in two phenomena—the first the behavior of Stromberg's shoelaces, which, as he strode back and forth, used to untie and drag like an Indian brave's travois. The second was the ballet he engaged in daily with his pipes. Not long before, in trying to break the cigarette habit, he had assembled a rack of the costliest pipes the tobacconists of two continents could furnish. There were stubby little briars covered in pigskin, meerschaums pre-colored by generations of Black Forest woodsmen, churchwardens that had belonged to the Stuarts, pipes with metal covers to be smoked in the rain while wearing veldtschoen shoes. Whenever a sudden craving for the weed halted his discourse, Stromberg would snatch up one of the pipes, ignite half a dozen wooden matches and fling them aside in a spectacular display of pyrotechnics, and puff till his cheeks empurpled. "I don't know—

I can't make these Goddam things work!" he would exclaim fretfully. None of our po-faced quartet felt it politic to suggest that a pinch of tobacco from his rosewood and mahogany humidors might help.

Our gauleiter's larynx having finally seized up from hyperactivity, we were released and wrote a treatment whose bromides made his seem paltry. Before we could begin the screenplay, though, real life obtruded on the world of make-believe: my wife's obstetrician learned that M-G-M had no lying-in facilities for an impending event and withdrew her from the combo. There was a fortnight's quest for a suitable collaborator, who, to our mutual astonishment, turned out to be another domestic team, Dorothy Parker and Alan Campbell. Since they were country neighbors, I moved swiftly to brief them on the taffy pull they were joining, but Stromberg was not to be denied the pleasure of bombinating to fresh faces, and a second three-day parley began.

While I narrowly escaped migraine from the repetition of all the platitudes, there was one compensation: it was piquant to observe how one's friends behaved in an industrial setting as contrasted with the drawing room. Mrs. Parker discharged no immortal epigrams or salty apothegms; she sat in a deep armchair, Churchillian glasses athwart her nose, knitting a gray artifact seven feet long that looked like a staircase runner and keeping her lip buttoned. Campbell was the drive train of the duo, toothy, voluble, bubbling with suggestions, charming the birds out of the trees. Stromberg roved to and fro, declaiming his guidelines and prose poems. Every so often, he would veer toward Mrs. Parker and address her with timid respect.

"I'd say we were making pretty good progress on the story, eh, Dorothy?"

Mrs. Parker would look up, plainly retrieving her attention from very far away, and reply with a hint of breathlessness, "Oh, I *do* think it's altogether marvelous, don't you?"

By the afternoon of the third day, I was plumb tuckered out, so I really wasn't wide-awake when it happened. I remember Stromberg's laces trailing across the carpet; I saw him fussing with his pipes and complaining; and I do recall kind of a mystifying nimbus swirling around Mrs. Parker's head that was not quite a halo. It was Campbell's piercing scream that wrenched me upward.

"Dottie!" he shrieked. "You're on fire!"

Well, she wasn't, actually—it was just kapok, the stuffing in her chair that was touched off by one of Stromberg's matches, and it smoked and smoldered a bit after we yanked her out and rolled her on the floor. People ran in, throwing Lily Cups of water on the cushions, but the damage was piffling. The damage to the chair, that is—the damage wrought by *Sweethearts* is still being dealt with by therapists, I presume. But they can hardly hold my wife and me responsible. God knows we had little enough to do with it.

III

One burning July afternoon in the late fifties, a violet-and-peach-colored object that was neither a flying saucer nor a sizzling platter but a twin-propellered Cessna materialized in the desert sky above the Palm Springs airport. Simultaneously, a violet-and-peach-colored Rolls-Royce piloted by a chauffeur in matching livery drew up at the terminal's arrival gate. In two shakes of a lamb's tail—the official signal for aircraft to land in Palm Springs—the plane had landed and a flourish of trumpets greeted its three passengers, two of whom were familiar to any bystander. They were the renowned *vedette* Elizabeth Taylor and her producer husband, Mike Todd. The third, who bore more than a passing resemblance to the *Apollo Belvedere* but could not be said, in all justice, to rank with him intellectually, was the present writer. His chief distinction—if one may borrow G. K. Chesterton's facility with paradox for a moment—was that he possessed no distinction whatsoever. What startling conjunction of the planets, therefore, what mysterious and inexplicable forces of the I Ching had mingled the destiny of this utter cipher with that of these eminent face cards? For the answer, the reader would have been obliged to wire-tap a trans-continental phone call between the celebrated showman and my literary agent, one Mark Hanna.

Mark Hanna was a rara avis, a saturnine, hyperbolic fashion plate who secretly believed that it took more talent to bushel a seam than to compose an ode to a skylark. With a rose tucked behind his ear, he could have had a fabulous career as Blazes Boylan in any production of *Ulysses in Nighttown* on earth, but he preferred to lounge in an out-at-elbows cardigan in his office and wrangle with his clients. His noontime call to me consisted of three simple declarative sentences.

"Mike Todd's just been on the blower from L.A.," he reported. "He says he can't eat, he can't sleep unless you sky out to discuss his next blockbuster, *Don Quixote*. In his book, you are the greatest writer since Danny Aligheri, the guy who wrote the *Inferno*."

"I once heard the same refrain played on a flute in Bombay," I said. "Someone was trying to lure a cobra out of a drain. What is all this leading up to?"

"A round trip economy-class to the Coast plus a tiny per diem. The man just wants to drop a few pebbles into your mind and see if it gives off the right kind of echo."

"In view of the man's affluence, to which I partially contributed in a previous blockbuster of his," I replied, "would you say that his offer is princely?"

"No, but coming from a former carnival hustler, it reminds one of the Medici. You know, son, you really should be more tolerant—we all of us have our deficiencies. You, for example—given a normal physique, you could be fulfilling your real talent today."

"And what is that?"

"Spading up potatoes on the North Fork of Long Island." There was an interval during which Hanna listened to the veins throbbing in my temples, and then he became truly avuncular. Why not treat Todd's proposal as a lark, a jamboree, a paid vacation in the sun? As my wrath ebbed, little beads of tolerance trickled in to fill the vacuum, and I yielded.

On reaching the Los Angeles airport, I was intercepted by a hireling of the impresario, bearing my name in a cleft stick, who marinated me for a couple of hours in a VIP lounge until the other occupants of the Cessna appeared. The mere rumor of Elizabeth Taylor, naturally, had produced crowds of idolaters like worshippers of Kali, moaning and twitching and scourging themselves with copies of *Confidential* and the works of Mrs. Aphra Behn. Todd, who fed on turbulence as on catnip, was in seventh heaven; he ordered batteries of phones plugged in, telexes to start clacking, outriders and emissaries to mill to and fro, and in the end a cuadrilla of police was required to escort us onto the airship. Somewhere in the course of the flight, I was apprised that we were bound for a desert hideaway sublet from Marion Davies, where Mike and I could rap undisturbed and Elizabeth could familiarize herself with Owen Johnson's Lawrenceville stories, in which she had been proposed for the twin roles of Doc MacNooder and the Tennessee Shad.

Our arrival at the *estancia* was almost as exciting as our take-off. Awaiting Elizabeth outside were her two sons by a prior marriage aged four and six respectively, in charge of a German nanny. While they were embracing, Mike rushed to the trunk of the car and burrowed inside. In a moment, he returned with an aluminum model of a naval destroyer or escort vessel about a yard long. A jewel of craftsmanship such as a retired admiral would treasure in his den, it must have cost at least nineteen thousand dollars at F. A. O. Schwarz.

"Look what Daddy's brought you!" Todd shouted at the boys. "Boom, boom! Come watch it work!"

The effect on the lads was hardly that intended: the younger fell to the ground howling in fright; the elder stared paralyzed at Mike, torn between curiosity and dread. Then, like a jump cut in film, the action switched abruptly to the swimming pool. The women and the smaller boy had vanished, and Mike, a cigar gripped in his teeth, stood tugging furiously on a string designed to operate the toy, his face contorted like a Japanese print. At length, whether it was his maledictions or the lighter fluid he kept spraying into it, labor, in accordance with the adage, vanquished all; there was an explosion and a hissing out of all relation to its size, and the craft shot away popping and snorting like an old sea dog. It went on ricocheting off the gutters and creating such hubbub that a gardener ultimately had to beat it with sticks till it subsided.

That evening the three of us drove into Chez Aloof, a restaurant staffed by very aloof Armenians, to dine with an octogenarian couple—East Coast plutocrats, I gathered—who owned a first edition of *Don Quixote* that Mike was angling to borrow for an establishing shot in the film. Just what the aged bibliophiles stood to gain from the transaction was unclear and was further diffused by wave after wave of Daiquiris that inundated us before the meal. I felt the grog beginning to shiver my timbers when I heard the old gentleman relating an occurrence at Lindy's in the twenties.

"I was lunching there that particular day with a friend of mine, a wide-wale-corduroy importer, when who should come in but this gambler, a party named Wolfsheim. He always wore cuff links made of human teeth."

"And hung around with the eponymous Jay Gatz," I added automatically.

"What did you say, young man?"

I shrugged. "Oh, nothing. I guess you also collect first editions of Scott Fitzgerald, don't you?"

"Listen, you," he said, grasping my necktie. "I'm eighty-nine years old, but I got a good mind to knock your block off."

"Just go ahead and try, old-timer," I dared him, and fell into a fighter's crouch like Battling Nelson's, which, inasmuch as I was sitting down, was not very ominous. "I'm a wide wale too, and I'm pretty handy with my flukes."

The dispute never reached the squared circle because everyone by then, the help included, was overcome by creeping aloofness and our party dissolved. The next morning, I arose early for a scheduled discussion of *Don Quixote*. The temperature was already in the nineties and the rest of the household was nowhere in evidence, but Todd was out by the pool, enmeshed in phone calls. Through the tie line in his New York offices, he was checking the foreign grosses of his blockbuster in Bulawayo, Dortmund, Nicosia, Juneau, and Stavanger, uttering mingled cries of jubilation and heartburn. Interthreaded with these were calls to his brokers, lawyers, press agents, backers, various casinos and racetracks, and stagefolk innumerable. At twelve forty-five he got up and stretched.

"That's all for now," he said. "Now, this aft I'm having some steam with Harry Cohn at the Racquet Club. There's milk and cookies for your lunch in the kitchen, and I'll be back at four ready for work, so stand by—do you hear? Don't goof off anywhere."

As the hours dragged by and the heat rose into the low hundreds, I began to feel mutinous. How insupportable that those two panjandrums should luxuriate in the steam while I sat on this marble bench at poolside frying myself into a plateful of goose cracklings. And how self-centered of Mike, how inconsiderate of him not to suggest some pastime to beguile the time. A more kindly nature would have invited me to gather the grass clippings, or to botanize the many interesting genera of cacti baking away in the gneiss outside the estate. . . . Oh, well, the devil with these ungenerous reflections; I would do far better to immerse myself in the paperback copy of *Don Quixote* my host had laid out for our meeting. So I did so literally, draping its pages over my crown to buffer it against the pitiless rays of Old Sol, and slept like a baby until Todd's voice aroused me. He was on the phone again, this time checking the blockbuster grosses in Cayenne, Windhoek, Djibouti, Vaduz, and Binghamton. It was dusk when he finished.

"About time you woke up, for Crissake," he said. "O.K., got the cobwebs out of your brain? What's the verdict?"

"About what?"

"The story—what do you think I'm talking about, the World Series? Does it excite you?"

"No, I wouldn't say it does that . . ."

"Then what does it do?"

"Oh, Mike," I pleaded. "Don't ask me that, please. Everything's been so perfect up to now . . ."

Todd removed his cigar and stared at me in alarm. "Say, what the hell's wrong with you?"

"Look," I said earnestly. "I hope what I'm about to say isn't going to affect our friendship. You didn't write the story and I didn't write the story. Cervantes wrote it, and he's not here." I cast a hurried glance about. "That is, I *say* he's not here, but who knows?"

"Goddam it, will you get to the point?"

"All right. The truth is, Mike, no matter how many times I've tried to read *Don Quixote*, I've never been able to get beyond page six. Indeed, so soporific is its effect that I believe it should be withdrawn from libraries everywhere and dispensed only on prescription."

He looked at me as though he had just bitten into a quince. "So that's your considered opinion, is it, wise guy?"

"No, a much wiser guy's. Aldous Huxley once called it the world's most unread classic."

Todd eyed me vindictively. "And I thought you were the only one on earth to do the screenplay. Well, thank God I found out in time, and not from you."

"Oh?" I said. "From who else?"

"Harry Cohn," he said. "He warned me in the steam. He heard that Universal let you go after two days."

Which shows how life always catches up with you.